GCSE

SUCCESS

MATHEMATICS

HIGHER

Author

Fiona C Mapp

CONTENTS

NUMBER

ALGEBRA

SHAPE, SPACE AND MEASURES

Revised

HANDLING DATA

Revised

TYPES OF NUMBERS

SQUARE ROOTS AND CUBE ROOTS

$\sqrt{}$ is the square root sign. Taking the square root is the opposite of squaring.
For example, $\sqrt{25} = 5$ since $5^2 = 25$, or $(-5)^2 = 25$.
$\sqrt[3]{}$ is the cube root sign. Taking the cube root is the opposite of cubing.
For example, $\sqrt[3]{8} = 2$ since $2^3 = 8$.

SQUARES AND CUBES

SQUARE NUMBERS

Anything to the <u>power 2</u> is <u>square</u>. For example, $6^2 = 6 \times 6 = 36$ (six squared).

Square numbers include:

1	4	9	16	25	36	49	64	81	100	. . .
(1 x 1)	(2 x 2)	(3 x 3)	(4 x 4)	(5 x 5)	(6 x 6)	(7 x 7)	(8 x 8)	(9 x 9)	(10 x 10)	

Square numbers can be illustrated by drawing squares:

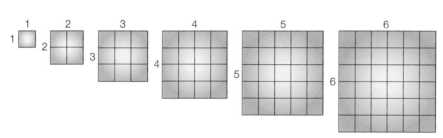

You need to know up to 15^2

CUBE NUMBERS

Anything to the <u>power 3</u> is <u>cube</u>. For example, $5^3 = 5 \times 5 \times 5 = 125$ (five cubed).
Cube numbers include:

1	8	27	64	125	216 . . .
(1 x 1 x 1)	(2 x 2 x 2)	(3 x 3 x 3)	(4 x 4 x 4)	(5 x 5 x 5)	(6 x 6 x 6)

Cube numbers can be illustrated by drawing cubes:

Examiner's Top Tip
It is important that you recognise square and cube numbers because they often appear in number sequences.

4

MULTIPLES

These are just the numbers in multiplication tables. For example, multiples of 8 are 8, 16, 24, 32, 40, . . .

RECIPROCALS

The reciprocal of a number $\frac{a}{x}$ is $\frac{x}{a}$ $(= x \div a)$. Multiplying a number by its reciprocal always gives 1.

EXAMPLES

• The reciprocal of $\frac{2}{3}$ is $\frac{3}{2}$.

• The reciprocal of 4 is $\frac{1}{4}$ because 4 is the same as $\frac{4}{1}$.

• To find the reciprocal of $1\frac{2}{3}$, first put it in the form a/x (so $1\frac{2}{3} = \frac{5}{3}$), and then invert it ($\frac{3}{5}$).

FACTORS AND PRIMES

FACTORS

These are whole numbers which <u>divide</u> <u>exactly</u> into another number. For example, the factors of 20 are

1, 2, 4, 5, 10, 20.

Factors of 20 can be split up into factor pairs.

So
1 x 20 = 20	
2 x 10 = 20	
4 x 5 = 20	

FACTORS
To find all the factors of a number, start at 1 and divide by each number in turn.

PRIME NUMBERS

These are numbers which have only two factors, <u>1</u> <u>and</u> <u>itself</u>. Note that 1 is <u>not</u> a prime number. Prime numbers up to 20 are

2, 3, 5, 7, 11, 13, 17, 19.

PRIME FACTORS

These are factors which are prime. Some numbers can be written as products of their prime factors.

EXAMPLE

The diagram below shows the prime factors of 360.

• Divide 360 by its first prime factor, 2.

• Divide 180 by its first prime factor, 2.

• Keep on going until the final number is prime.

<u>As a product of its prime factors</u> <u>360</u> <u>may be written as:</u>

$2 \times 2 \times 2 \times 3 \times 3 \times 5 = 360$

or $2^3 \times 3^2 \times 5 = 360$

in index notation (using powers).

HIGHEST COMMON FACTOR (HCF)

The <u>largest</u> <u>factor</u> that two numbers have in common is called the <u>HCF</u>.

EXAMPLE

Find the HCF of 84 and 360.

• Write the numbers as products of their prime factors.

$84 = 2 \times 2 \times 3 \times 7$
$360 = 2 \times 2 \times 2 \times 3 \times 3 \times 5$

• Ring the factors in common

• These give the HCF $= 2 \times 2 \times 3 = 12$

LOWEST COMMON MULTIPLE (LCM)

This is the <u>lowest</u> number which is a <u>multiple</u> of two numbers.

EXAMPLE

Find the LCM of 6 and 8.

• Write the numbers as products of their prime factors.

• $8 = 2 \times 2 \times 2$

• $6 = 2 \times 3$

• 8 and 6 have a common prime factor of 2. So it is only counted once.

• The LCM of 6 and 8 is $2 \times 2 \times 2 \times 3 = 24$

QUICK TEST

1. List the prime numbers up to 20.

2. Find the HCF and LCM of 24 and 60.

3. Find a) $\sqrt{64}$ b) $\sqrt[3]{216}$

4. Write down the reciprocals of a) $\frac{9}{12}$ b) $\frac{x}{p}$

POSITIVE & NEGATIVE NUMBERS

NEGATIVE ← **POSITIVE** →

–10 –9 –8 –7 –6 –5 –4 –3 –2 –1 0 1 2 3 4 5 6 7 8 9 10

GETTING SMALLER   GETTING BIGGER

DIRECTED NUMBERS

These are numbers which may be <u>positive</u> or <u>negative</u>.
Positive are above zero, negative are below zero.

EXAMPLES
–10 is smaller than –8.   –10 < –8
–4 is bigger than –8.   –4 > –8
2 is bigger than –6.   2 > –6

Directed numbers are often seen on the weather
forecast in winter. Quite often the temperature is below 0.
Aberdeen is the coldest at –8°C.
London is 6°C warmer than Manchester.

-8 Aberdeen
-4 Manchester
2 London

INTEGERS

The integers are the set of numbers {. . ., –3, –2, –1, 0, 1, 2, 3, . . .}.
When referring to integers, the term <u>integral</u> <u>value</u> is used. A number
that is <u>non–integral</u> is not an integer.

MULTIPLYING AND DIVIDING DIRECTED NUMBERS

<u>Multiply</u> <u>and</u> <u>divide</u> <u>the</u> <u>numbers</u> <u>as</u> <u>normal.</u>
<u>Then</u> <u>find</u> <u>the</u> <u>sign</u> <u>for</u> <u>the</u> <u>answer</u> <u>using</u> <u>these</u> <u>rules:</u>

- **two <u>like</u> signs (both + or both –) give positive,**
- **two <u>unlike</u> signs (one + and the other –)**
  give negative.

(+) x (+) = +
(–) x (–) = +
(+) x (–) = –
(–) x (+) = –

(+) ÷ (+) = +
(–) ÷ (–) = +
(+) ÷ (–) = –
(–) ÷ (+) = –

EXAMPLES
–6 x (+4) = –24   –12 ÷ (–3) = 4
–6 x (–3) = 18   20 ÷ (–4) = –5

Examiner's Top Tip
The rules of multiplication/
division need to be
remembered. You could
quite easily use these laws
when multiplying out
brackets in algebra.

ADDING AND SUBTRACTING DIRECTED NUMBERS

EXAMPLE
The temperature at 6 a.m. was –5°C. By 10 a.m. it had risen 8 degrees. So the new temperature was 3°C.

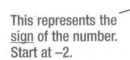

+ 8
Start ⌢⌢⌢⌢⌢⌢⌢⌢ Finish
–5 –4 –3 –2 –1 0 1 2 3 4

EXAMPLE
Find the value of –2 – 4.

–2 – 4

This represents the <u>sign</u> of the number. Start at –2.

This represents the operation of <u>subtraction</u>. Move 4 places to the left.

–4
Finish ⌢⌢⌢⌢ Start
–6 –5 –4 –3 –2 –1 0 1 2 3 4

So –2 – 4 = –6
When the number to be added (or subtracted) is <u>negative</u>, the normal direction of movement is <u>reversed</u>.

EXAMPLE   –4 – (–3) is the same as –4 + 3 = –1

The negative changes the <u>direction</u>.   **Move 3 places to the <u>right</u>.**

When two (+) or two (–) signs are together, these rules are used:

+(+) → +
–(–) → + } like signs give a <u>positive</u>,

+(–) → –
–(+) → – } unlike signs give a <u>negative</u>.

EXAMPLES
–6 + (–2) = –6 – 2 = –8   –2 – (+6) = –2 – 6 = –8
4 – (–3) = 4 + 3 = 7   9 + (–3) = 9 – 3 = 6

Examiner's Top Tip
If you find working with directed numbers difficult, sketch a quick number line to help you.

NEGATIVE NUMBERS ON THE CALCULATOR

The +/– or (–) key on the calculator gives a <u>negative</u> number.
For example, to get –6, press 6 +/– or
(–) 6 .
This represents the <u>sign</u>.

EXAMPLE
–4 – (–2) = –2
is keyed in the calculator like this:

4   +/–   –   2   +/–   =
     ↑   ↑   ↑
    sign operation sign

Make sure you know how to enter negative numbers in <u>your</u> calculator.

QUICK TEST

1. If the temperature was –12°C at 2 a.m., and it rose by 15 degrees by 11 a.m., what was the temperature at 11 a.m.?

2. Work these out, without a calculator.

   a) –2 – (–6)   b) –9 + (–7)   c) –2 × 6

   d) –9 + (–3)   e) –20 ÷ (–4)   f) –18 ÷ (–3)

   g) 4 – (–3)   h) –7 + (–3)   i) –9 × –4

1. 3°C   2. a) 4 b) –16 c) –12 d) –12 e) 5 f) 6 g) 7 h) –10 i) 36

EQUIVALENT FRACTIONS

These are fractions which have the same value.

EXAMPLE

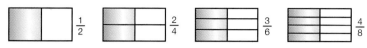

$\frac{1}{2}$ $\frac{2}{4}$ $\frac{3}{6}$ $\frac{4}{8}$

From the diagrams it can be seen that $\frac{1}{2} = \frac{2}{4} = \frac{3}{6} = \frac{4}{8}$.
They are <u>equivalent</u> <u>fractions</u>. Fractions can be changed
to their equivalent by <u>multiplying</u> or <u>dividing</u> both the
numerator and denominator by the same amount.

EXAMPLES

Change $\frac{5}{7}$ to its equivalent fraction with
a denominator of 28.

Multiply top and bottom by 4.
So $\frac{20}{28}$ is equivalent to $\frac{5}{7}$.

Change $\frac{40}{60}$ to its equivalent fraction with
a denominator of 3.

Divide top and bottom by 20.
So $\frac{40}{60}$ is equivalent to $\frac{2}{3}$.

Using the fraction key on the calculator

a% is the fraction key on the calculator.

EXAMPLE

$^{12}/_{18}$ is keyed in as `1` `2` `a%` `1` `8`
This is displayed as `12⌐8⌐18`
or `12⌐8⌐18`.
The calculator will automatically
cancel down fractions when the
`=` key is pressed. For example,
$^{12}/_{18}$ becomes `2⌐3` or `2⌐3`.
<u>This</u> <u>means</u> <u>two-thirds</u>
A display of `1⌐8⌐489` means 1%.
If you now press **shift** **a%**, it
converts back to an improper
fraction, `13⌐89`

MULTIPLICATION AND DIVISION OF FRACTIONS

When multiplying and dividing fractions, write out whole or mixed numbers as improper fractions before starting.

EXAMPLE

$\frac{2}{9} \times \frac{4}{7} = \frac{2 \times 4}{9 \times 7} = \frac{8}{63}$ ⟵ Multiply numerators together.
                                  ⟵ Multiply denominators together.

Change a division into a multiplication by turning the second
fraction upside down and multiplying both fractions together;
that is, <u>multiply</u> <u>by</u> <u>the</u> <u>reciprocal</u>.

EXAMPLE

$\frac{7}{9} \div \frac{12}{18} = \frac{7}{9} \times \frac{18}{12}$ Take the <u>reciprocal</u>
                     of the <u>second</u> <u>fraction</u>.

$= \frac{126}{108} = 1\frac{1}{6}$ Rewrite the answer
                as a mixed number.

PROPORTIONAL CHANGES WITH FRACTIONS AND PERCENTAGES

INCREASE AND DECREASE

There are two methods. Use the one that is familiar to you.

EXAMPLE

Last year there were 290 people belonging to a gym. This year there are $\frac{3}{5}$ more. How many people now belong?

> Remember 'of' means multiply

METHOD 1

$\frac{3}{5} \times 290 = 174$
$290 + 174 = 464$ people

Work out $\frac{3}{5}$ of 290.
Add this on to the original number.

METHOD 2

Increasing by $\frac{3}{5}$ is the same as multiplying by
$1\frac{3}{5}$ ($1 + \frac{3}{5}$).
$1\frac{3}{5} \times 290 = 464$
On the calculator key in   `1` `a%` `3` `a%` `5` `x` `290` `=`

Use the fraction key to work this out, if possible. If this question is on the non-calculator paper, remember to:
- Divide 290 by the denominator $290 \div 5 = 58$ • Multiply by the numerator $58 \times 3 = 174$
- Now add onto the original value

ADDITION AND SUBTRACTION OF FRACTIONS

These examples show the basic principles of adding and subtracting fractions.

EXAMPLE

$\frac{1}{8} + \frac{3}{4}$

$\overset{\times 2}{\frac{3}{4} = \frac{6}{8}}\underset{\times 2}{}$

- First make the denominators the same: $\frac{3}{4} = \frac{6}{8}$

$\frac{3}{4}$ is **equivalent** to $\frac{6}{8}$.

$= \frac{1}{8} + \frac{6}{8}$ • Replace $\frac{3}{4}$ with $\frac{6}{8}$ so that the denominators are the same.

$= \frac{7}{8}$ • Add the numerators $1 + 6 = 7$. **Do not add** the denominators; the denominator stays the same number.

EXAMPLE

$\frac{9}{12} - \frac{1}{3}$

$\overset{\times 4}{\frac{1}{3} = \frac{4}{12}}\underset{\times 4}{}$

- First make the denominators the same: $\frac{1}{3} = \frac{4}{12}$
  $\frac{1}{3}$ is equivalent to $\frac{4}{12}$.

$= \frac{9}{12} - \frac{4}{12}$ • Replace the $\frac{1}{3}$ with $\frac{4}{12}$.

$= \frac{5}{12}$ • Subtract the numerators but **not** the denominators; the denominator stays the same number.

On a calculator you would type in:

| 9 | a% | 12 | – | 1 | a% | 3 | = |

FRACTIONS

A fraction is a part of a whole one. $\frac{4}{5}$ means 4 parts out of 5.
The top number is the numerator. The bottom one is the denominator.

A fraction like $\frac{4}{5}$ is called a proper fraction.
A fraction like $\frac{24}{17}$ is called an improper fraction.
$2\frac{1}{2}$ is called a mixed number.

QUICK TEST

1. Without using a calculator work out the following:

a) $\frac{2}{9} + \frac{3}{27}$ b) $\frac{3}{5} - \frac{1}{4}$

c) $\frac{6}{9} \times \frac{72}{104}$ d) $\frac{8}{9} \div \frac{2}{3}$

e) $\frac{4}{7} - \frac{1}{3}$ f) $\frac{2}{7} \div 1\frac{1}{2}$

g) $\frac{7}{11} \div \frac{22}{14}$ h) $\frac{2}{9} + \frac{4}{7}$

2. Calculate $\frac{2}{9}$ of £180.

3. $\frac{7}{12}$ more rain fell this year. If 156 mm fell last year, how much fell this year?

Examiner's Top Tip
Questions involving fractions are quite common on the non-calculator paper. Learn the quick way of finding a fraction of a quantity.

1. a) $\frac{1}{3}$ b) $\frac{7}{20}$ c) $\frac{6}{13}$ d) $1\frac{1}{3}$ e) $\frac{5}{21}$ f) $\frac{4}{21}$ g) $\frac{49}{121}$ h) $\frac{50}{63}$ 2. £40   3. 247 mm

DECIMALS

DECIMAL PLACES (D.P.)

When rounding numbers to a specified number of decimal places:
- look at the last number that is wanted (if rounding 12.367 to 2 d.p., look at the 6 which is the second d.p.);
- look at the number to the right of it (look at the number which is not needed – the 7);
- if it is 5 or more, then round up the last digit (7 is greater than 5, so round up the 6 to a 7);
- if it is less than 5, then the digit remains the same;

EXAMPLES

Round 12.49 to 1 d.p.
12.49 rounds up to 12.5.

Round 8.735 to 2 d.p.
8.735 rounds up to 8.74.

Round 9.624 to 2 d.p.
9.624 rounds to 9.62

12.49
12.4   12.45   12.5

8.735
8.73   8.735   8.74

9.624
9.62   9.625   9.63

ORDERING DECIMALS

When ordering decimals:
- first write them with the same number of figures after the decimal point;
- then compare whole numbers, digits in the tenths place, digits in the hundredths place, and so on.

EXAMPLES

Arrange these numbers in order of size, smallest first:
6.21, 6.023, 6.4, 6.04, 2.71, 9.4
First rewrite them:
6.210, 6.023, 6.400, 6.040, 2.710, 9.400
Then re-order them:
2.710, 6.023, 6.040, 6.210, 6.400, 9.400

> Remember, hundredths are smaller than tenths
> $\frac{10}{100} = \frac{1}{10}$ so $\frac{6}{100} < \frac{1}{10}$

CALCULATIONS WITH DECIMALS

When adding and subtracting decimals, the decimal points need to go under each other.

EXAMPLES

27.46
7.291 +
34.751
1 1

> • Line up the digits carefully

$\overset{6\ 9\ 1}{17.\cancel{0}0}$
12.84 –
4.16

> • The decimal point in the answer will be in line

> • Put the decimal points under each other

When multiplying decimals, the answer must have the same number of decimal places as the total number of decimal places in the numbers which are being multiplied.

EXAMPLES

24.6
7 x
172.2
3 4

> • Remember to check with your calculator

Multiply 246 by 7 = 1722, ignoring the decimal point. 24.6 has 1 number after the decimal point. The answer must have 1 decimal place (1 d.p.).

So 24.6 x 7 = 172.2

Work out 4.52 x 0.2

452
2 x
904
1

Work out 452 x 2, ignoring the decimal points. 4.52 has 2 d.p. 0.2 has 1 d.p. So the answer must have 3 d.p.

904 ➡ 0.904   Move the decimal point 3 places.

So 4.52 x 0.2 = 0.904

When dividing decimals, divide as normal, placing the decimal points in line.

EXAMPLE

$3\overline{)1^{1}4.^{2}4}$ 4.8

> Put the decimal points in line.

A decimal point is used to separate whole number columns from fractional columns.

EXAMPLE

Thousands	Hundreds	Tens	Units	.	Tenths	Hundredths	Thousandths
5	9	2	4	.	1	6	3

Decimal Point

• The 1 means $\frac{1}{10}$. • The 6 means $\frac{6}{100}$. • The 3 means $\frac{3}{1000}$.

RECURRING DECIMALS

A decimal that recurs is shown by placing a dot over the numbers that repeat.

EXAMPLES

$0.333\ldots = 0.\dot{3}$ $0.17777\ldots = 0.1\dot{7}$ $0.232323\ldots = 0.\dot{2}\dot{3}$

MULTIPLYING AND DIVIDING BY NUMBERS BETWEEN 0 AND 1

When <u>multiplying</u> by numbers between 0 and 1, the result is <u>smaller</u> than the starting value.
When <u>dividing</u> by numbers between 0 and 1, the result is <u>bigger</u> than the starting value.

EXAMPLES

$6 \times 0.1 = 0.6$

$6 \times 0.01 = 0.06$

$6 \times 0.001 = 0.006$

The result is smaller than the starting value.

$6 \div 0.1 = 60$

$6 \div 0.01 = 600$

$6 \div 0.001 = 6000$

The result is bigger than the starting value.

QUICK TEST

1. Without using a calculator work out the following:

   a) 27.16 + 9.32   b) 29.04 – 11.361   c) 12.8 x 2.1

   d) 49.2 ÷ 4   e) 600 x 0.01   f) 520 x 0.1

   g) 20 x 0.02   h) 37 x 0.0001   i) 400 ÷ 0.1

   j) 450 ÷ 0.01   k) 470 ÷ 0.001   l) 650 ÷ 0.02

2. Round the following numbers to 2 decimal places:

   a) 7.469

   b) 12.0372

   c) 9.365

   d) 10.042

   e) 8.1794

Examiner's Top Tip
Multiplying and dividing by numbers between 0 and 1 usually occur on the non-calculator paper – it is wise to practise these by writing out several calculations and then checking the answer with a calculator.

2. a) 7.47 b) 12.04 c) 9.37 d) 10.04 e) 8.18
1. a) 36.48 b) 17.679 c) 26.88 d) 12.3 e) 6 f) 52 g) 0.4 h) 0.0037 i) 4000 j) 45000 k) 470000 l) 32500

PERCENTAGE OF A QUANTITY

The word '**of**' means **multiply**. For example,
40% of £600 becomes $\frac{40}{100}$ x 600 = £240
On the calculator key in
40 ÷ 100 x 600 =
If this is on the non-calculator paper
• Work out 10% first by dividing by 10
   e.g. 600 ÷10 = £60.
• Multiply by 4 to get 40% i.e. 4 x 60 = £240.

Examiner's Top Tip
Percentage questions appear frequently at GCSE. If there is a percentage question on the non-calculator paper, try and work out what 10% is equal to, as shown in the examples above.

This is just like a percentage of a quantity question.

EXAMPLE
A meal for four costs £92.20. VAT is charged at 17.5%.
• VAT is a tax which is added on to the cost of most items.
a) How much VAT is there to pay on the meal?
b) What is the final price of the meal?

a) 17.5% of £92.20
= $\frac{17.5}{100}$ x 92.20 = £16.14
(to the nearest penny)
VAT = £16.14
b) Price of meal = £92.20 + £16.14 = £108.34

An alternative is to use a scale factor method.
• an increase of 17.5%, is the same as multiplying by 1 + $\frac{17.5}{100}$ = 1.175.
£92.20 x 1.175 = £108.34 (to the nearest penny).

Value added tax (VAT)

PERCENTAGES ①

THESE ARE FRACTIONS WITH A DENOMINATOR OF 100
% IS THE PERCENTAGE SIGN.
75% MEANS $\frac{75}{100}$ (THIS IS ALSO EQUAL TO $\frac{3}{4}$).

75%

PERCENTAGE INCREASE AND DECREASE

The answer will be a percentage so multiply by 100%.

% change = $\frac{change}{original}$ x 100%

EXAMPLE
A coat costs £125. In a sale it is reduced to £85.
What is the percentage reduction?
Reduction = £125 – £85 = £40
$\frac{40}{125}$ x 100% = 32%

EXAMPLE
Matthew bought a flat for £45000.
Three years later, he sold it for £62000.
What was his percentage profit?
Profit = £62000 – £45000
= £17000
% Profit = $\frac{17000}{45000}$ x 100% = 37.78%

ONE QUANTITY AS A PERCENTAGE OF ANOTHER

To make the answer a <u>percentage</u>, multiply by <u>100%</u>.

EXAMPLE

In a carton of milk, 6.2 g of the contents are fat.
If 2.5 g of the fat is saturated, what percentage is this?
$\frac{2.5}{6.2} \times 100\% = 40.3\%$ (to 1 d.p.)
On the calculator key in
2.5 ÷ 6.2 × 100 =

Multiply by 100% to get a percentage.

$$\text{Fraction} \xrightarrow{\times 100\%} \text{Percentage}$$

REVERSE PERCENTAGE PROBLEMS

Reverse percentage is when the <u>original quantity</u> is calculated.

EXAMPLE

The price of a television is reduced by 20% in the sales.
It <u>now</u> costs £250. What was the original price?

- The sale price is 100% − 20% = 80% of the pre-sale price.
    $\frac{80}{100} = 0.8$
    0.8 × (price) = £250
    price = 250/0.8 = £312.50

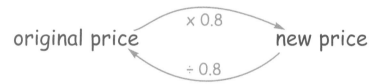

$$\text{original price} \underset{\div 0.8}{\overset{\times 0.8}{\rightleftharpoons}} \text{new price}$$

80%

It is 80% of the original price which is being found, not 80% of the new one.

- Always check the answer is sensible.
- Is the original price more than the sale price?

QUICK TEST

1. Work out 30% of £700.

2. Sarah got 94 out of 126 in a Maths test. What percentage did she get?

3. Reece weighed 6 lb when he was born. If his weight has increased by 65%, how much does he now weigh?

4. The price of a hi-fi is reduced by 15% in the sales. It now costs £350. What was the original price?

5.

Super's football boots	Joe's football boots
$\frac{1}{3}$ off	28% off

If a pair of football boots costs £49.99, which shop sells them cheaper in the sale and what is the price?

REPEATED PERCENTAGE CHANGE

EXAMPLE
A car was bought for £8000 in 1994. Each year it depreciated in value by 20%. What is the car worth 3 years later?

Work these questions out year by year.

METHOD 1
• Find 80% of the value of the car first.
  Year 1 $\frac{80}{100}$ x £8000 = £6400
• Then work out the value year by year.
  Year 2 $\frac{80}{100}$ x £6400 = £5120 (£6400 depreciates in value by 20%.)
  Year 3 $\frac{80}{100}$ x £5120 = £4096 after 3 years (£5120 depreciates by 20%.)

Beware: do not do 3 x 20 = 60% reduction over 3 years!

METHOD 2
• A quick way to work this out uses the scale factor method.
• Finding 80% of the value of the car is the same as multiplying by 0.8. 0.8 is the scale factor.
  Year 1   0.8 x £8000 = £6400
  Year 2   0.8 x £6400 = £5120
  Year 3   0.8 x £5120 = £4096
This is the same as working out $(0.8)^3$ x 8000 = £4096
A much quicker way if you understand it!

SIMPLE INTEREST

This is the interest that is sometimes paid on money in banks and building societies. The interest is paid each year (per annum or p.a.) and is the same amount each year.

EXAMPLE
Jonathan has £2500 in his savings account. Simple interest is paid at 4.4% p.a. How much does he have in his account at the end of the year?

This is a 'percentage of' question

100 + 4.4 = 104.4% (increasing by 4.4% is the same as multiplying by 100 + 44 = 104.4 %)
Total savings = $\frac{104.4}{100}$ x £2500 = £2610
Interest paid = £2610 – £2500 = £110

Note: If the money was in the account for 4 years, the interest at the end of the 4 years would be 4 x £110 = £440

COMPOUND INTEREST

This is the type of interest where the bank pays interest on the interest earned as well as on the original money.

EXAMPLE
If Jonathan has £2500 in his savings account and compound interest is paid at 4.4% p.a., how much will he have in his account after 4 years?

METHOD 1
Year 1: $\frac{104.4}{100}$ x £2500 = £2610
Year 2: 1.044 x £2610 = £2724.84
Year 3: 1.044 x £2724.84 = £2844.73
Year 4: 1.044 x £2844.73 = £2969.90
Total = £2969.90 (nearest penny)

METHOD 2
$\frac{104.4}{100}$ = 1.044 is the scale factor
£2500 x 1.044 x 1.044 x 1.044 x 1.044
= 2500 x $(1.044)^4$
Total = £2969.90 (nearest penny)

Method 2 uses the scale factor method

14

TAX AND NATIONAL INSURANCE

NATIONAL INSURANCE
National Insurance (NI) is usually deducted as a percentage from a wage.

EXAMPLE
Sue earns £1402.65 a month. National Insurance at 9% is deducted. How much NI must she pay?
9% of £1402.65 = 0.09 x £1402.65 = £126.24

INCOME TAX
A percentage of a wage or salary is removed as income tax.
Personal allowances must first be removed in order to obtain the taxable income.

EXAMPLE
Harold earns £190 per week. His first £62 is not
taxable but the remainder is taxed at 24%.
How much income tax does he pay each week?
Taxable income = £190 − £62 = £128
24% tax = 0.24 x £128 = £30.72
Tax per week = £30.72

Examiner's Top Tip
Being able to answer questions like the examples shown in this section is important – not only because they appear on the examination paper but because you will come across them in everyday life. Most of the examples are 'percentage of' questions.

PERCENTAGES ②

There are really only 2 types of percentage questions:

1. 'Percentage of'

Here you are given the percentage so you ÷ 100

2. Writing your answer as a percentage

Here you need to work out a percentage so you X 100

QUICK TEST

1. Charlotte has £4250 in the bank. If the interest rate is 6.8% p.a., how much interest on the savings will she get at the end of the year?

2. A car costs £6000 cash or can be bought by hire purchase with a 30% deposit followed by 12 monthly instalments of £365. Find:
   a) the deposit
   b) the total amount paid for the car on hire purchase

3. A flat was bought in 1998 for £62000. In 1999 the price increased by 20% and then by a further 35% in 2000. How much was the flat worth at the end of 2000?

4. Fiona has £3200 savings. If compound interest is paid at 3% p.a., how much will she have in her account after 3 years?

1. £289 2 a) £1800 b) £6180 3. £100440 4. £3496.73

EQUIVALENCES BETWEEN FRACTIONS, DECIMALS AND PERCENTAGES

FRACTIONS TO DECIMALS TO PERCENTAGES

Fractions, decimals and percentages all mean the same thing but are just written in a different way.

Fraction	Decimal	Percentage
$\frac{1}{2}$	0.5	50%
$\frac{1}{3}$	0.33	33.3%
$\frac{2}{3}$	0.66	66.6%
$\frac{1}{4}$	0.25	25%
$\frac{3}{4}$	0.75	75%
$\frac{1}{5}$	0.2	20%
$\frac{1}{8}$	0.125	12.5%
$\frac{3}{8}$	0.375	37.5%
$\frac{1}{10}$	0.1	10%
$\frac{1}{100}$	0.01	1%

$3 \div 4$ → ← x 100%

The above table shows
• Some common fractions and their equivalents which you need to learn.
• How to convert fractions ⟶ decimals ⟶ percentages.

ORDERING DIFFERENT NUMBERS

When putting fractions, decimals and percentages in order of size, it is best to change them all to decimals first.

EXAMPLE

$\frac{3}{5}$, 0.65, 0.273, 27%, 62%, $\frac{4}{9}$ ← Place in order of size, smallest first

0.6, 0.65, 0.273, 0.27, 0.62, 0.4̇4̇ ← Put into decimals first

0.27, 0.273, 0.4̇4̇, 0.6, 0.62, 0.65 ← Now order

Examiner's Top Tip
Get a friend to test you on the equivalences between fractions, decimals and percentages as you need to learn them.

QUICK TEST

1. Change the following fractions into a) decimals b) percentages

i) $\frac{2}{7}$ ii) $\frac{3}{5}$ iii) $\frac{8}{9}$

2. Place in order of size, smallest first:

$\frac{2}{5}$, 0.42, 0.041, $\frac{1}{3}$, 5%, 26%

1. i)a) 0.2857 b) 28.57% (2 d.p.) ii)a) 0.6 b) 60% iii)a) 0.88 b) 88.88%   2. 0.041, 5%, 26%, $\frac{1}{3}$, $\frac{2}{5}$, 0.42

USING A CALCULATOR

IMPORTANT CALCULATOR KEYS

This calculator is an imaginary one to show you some of the most important keys. Make sure you are familiar with your own calculator.

Practise using your own calculator. Make sure you know where these keys are

Shift or 2nd or Inv allow 2nd functions to be carried out.

allows a fraction to be put in the calculator

– or +/- changes positive numbers to negative ones

bracket keys

often puts the x10 part in when working in standard form.

pressing shift EXP often gives π

square root

square button

trigonometric buttons

memory keys

works out powers

cancels only the last key you have pressed

all memory keys

EXAMPLE

$\dfrac{15 \times 10 + 46}{9.3 \times 2.1} = 10.04$ (2 d.p.)

This may be keyed in as:
[(... 15 × 10 + 46 ...)] ÷ [(... 9.3 × 2.1 ...)] =

The above could be as easily done using the memory keys. Try writing down the key sequence for yourself.

CALCULATING POWERS

y^x or x^y is used for calculating powers such as 2^7.

• Use the power key on the calculator to work out 2^7.
• Write down calculator keys used.
• Check that you obtain the answer 128.
Now try writing down the keys that would be needed for these calculations.
Check that you get the right answers.

a) $\dfrac{2.9 \times 3.6}{(4.2 + 3.7)} = 1.322$ b) $9^{\frac{1}{3}} \times 4^5 = 2130$ c) $\dfrac{3 \times (5.2)^2}{9.6 \times (12.4)^3} = 4.432 \times 10^{-3}$

Examiner's Top Tip
Make sure you know how to use the power key as it saves lots of time.

QUICK TEST

Work these out on your calculator:

a) $\dfrac{27.1 \times 6.4}{9.3 + 2.7}$ b) $\dfrac{(9.3)^4}{2.7 \times 3.6}$

c) $\sqrt{\dfrac{25^2}{4\pi}}$ d) $\frac{5}{9}(25 - 10)$

a) 14.45 (2 d.p.)   b) 769.6 (1 d.p.)   c) 7.052 (3 d.p.)   d) 8 $\frac{1}{3}$ or 8.3̇

17

SIGNIFICANT FIGURES (S.F. OR SIG. FIG.)

Apply the same rule as with decimal places: if the next digit is 5 or more, round up. The 1st significant figure is the first digit which is not zero. The 2nd, 3rd, 4th,.... significant figures follow on after the 1st digit. They may or may not be zeros.

EXAMPLES

6.4027 has 5 s.f.
1st 2nd 3rd 4th 5th

0.0004701 has 4 s.f.
1st 2nd 3rd 4th

> Take care when rounding that you do not change the place values.

EXAMPLES

Number	to 3 s.f.	to 2 s.f.	to 1 s.f.
4.207	4.21	4.2	4
4379	4380	4400	4000
0.006209	0.00621	0.0062	0.006

After rounding the last digit, you must fill in the end zeros.
For example, 4380 = 4400 to 2 s.f. (not 44).

ESTIMATES AND APPROXIMATIONS

Estimating is a good way of checking answers.
• Round the numbers to 'easy' numbers, usually 1 or 2 significant figures.
• Work out the estimate using these easy numbers.
• Use the symbol ≈, which means 'approximately equal to'.
For multiplying or dividing, never approximate a number with zero.
Use 0.1, 0.01, 0.001, etc.

EXAMPLES

a) $8.93 \times 25.09 \approx 10 \times 25 = 250$

b) $(6.29)^2 \approx 6^2 = 36$

c) $\dfrac{296 \times 52.1}{9.72 \times 1.14} \approx \dfrac{300 \times 50}{10 \times 1} = \dfrac{15000}{10} = 1500$

d) $0.096 \times 79.2 \approx 0.1 \times 80 = 8$

EXAMPLE

Jack does the calculation $\dfrac{9.6 \times 103}{(2.9)^2}$

a) Estimate the answer to this calculation, without using a calculator.

b) Jack's answer is 1175.7. Is this the right order of magnitude?

a) Estimate $\dfrac{9.6 \times 103}{(2.9)^2} \approx \dfrac{10 \times 100}{3^2} = \dfrac{1000}{9} \approx \dfrac{1000}{10} = 100$

b) Jack's answer is not the right order of magnitude. It is 10 times too big.

When adding and subtracting, very small numbers may be approximated to zero.

EXAMPLES

$109.6 + 0.0002 \approx 110 + 0 = 110$ $63.87 - 0.01 \approx 64 - 0 = 64$

> **Examiner's Top Tip**
> Questions which involve approximating are common on the non-calculator paper. For most of these questions, you are expected to round to 1 significant figure. Even if you find the calculation difficult, show your approximations to help pick up method marks.

> **Right order of magnitude means 'about the right size'**

CHECKING CALCULATIONS

When checking calculations, the process can be reversed like this.

$\div 5$

3695   739

$\times 5$

EXAMPLE

$106 \times 3 = 318$
Check: $318 \div 3 = 106$

$\times 3$

106   318

$\div 3$

APPROXIMATING & CHECKING CALCULATIONS

CALCULATIONS

When solving problems the answers should be rounded sensibly.

Round to 2 d.p. because the values in the question are to 2 d.p.

EXAMPLE
$95.26 \times 6.39 = 608.7114 = 608.71$ (2 d.p.)

EXAMPLE
Jackie has £9.37. She divides it equally between 5 people. How much does each person receive?
$£9.37 \div 5 = £1.874$
         $= £1.87$

Round to 1.87 as it is money

EXAMPLE
Paint is sold in 8 litre tins. Sandra needs 27 litres of paint. How many tins must she buy?
$27 \div 8 = 3$ remainder 3
Sandra needs 4 tins of paint.
Sandra would not have enough paint with 3 tins, since she is 3 litres short. Hence the number of tins of paint must be rounded up.

When rounding remainders, consider the context of the question.

You will lose marks if you do not write money to 2 d.p. If the answer to a money calculation is £9.7, _always_ write it to 2 d.p. as £9.70.

QUICK TEST

1. Round the following numbers to 3 significant figures (3 s.f.):

   a) 0.003786   b) 27490   c) 307250

2. Estimate the answer to $\dfrac{(29.4)^2 + 106}{2.2 \times 5.1}$

3. Sukvinder decided to decorate her living room. The total area of the walls was 48 m². If one roll of wallpaper covers 5 m² of wall, how many rolls of wallpaper did Sukvinder need?

4. Thomas earned £109.25 for working a 23-hour week. How much was he paid per hour? Check your calculation by estimating.

SHARING A QUANTITY IN A GIVEN RATIO

- Add up the total parts.
- Work out what one part is worth.
- Work out what the other parts are worth.

EXAMPLE

£20 000 is shared in the ratio 1 : 4 between Ewan and Leroy.
How much does each receive?

1 + 4 = 5 parts

5 parts = £20 000

1 part = $\dfrac{£20\,000}{5}$ = £4000

So Ewan gets 1 x £4000 = £4000 and Leroy gets 4 x £4000 = £16 000.

INCREASING AND DECREASING IN A GIVEN RATIO

- **Divide to get one part.**
- **Multiply for each new part.**

EXAMPLE

A photograph of length 9 cm is to be enlarged in the ratio 5 : 3.
What is the length of the enlarged photograph?

- *Divide 9 cm by 3 to get 1 part.*

  9 ÷ 3 = 3

- *Multiply this by 5. So 5 x 3 = 15 cm on the*
  enlarged photograph.

9 cm

3 3 3

15 cm

3 3 3 3 3

EXAMPLE

A house took 8 people 6 days to build.
At the same rate how long would it take 3 people?
Time for 8 people = 6 days.
Time for 1 person = 8 x 6 = 48 days.
It takes 1 person longer to build the house.
Time for 3 people = $\dfrac{48}{3}$ = 16 days.
3 people will take $\dfrac{1}{3}$ of the time taken by 1 person.

EXAMPLE

A recipe for 4 people needs 1600 g of flour.
How much is needed for 6 people?

- *Divide 1600 g by 4, so 400 g for 1 person.*
- *Multiply by 6, so 6 x 400 g = 2400 g for*
  6 people.

FLOUR

Examiner's Top Tip
When answering problems of the type shown here always try and work out what a unit (or one) is worth. You should then be able to work out what any other value is worth.

BEST BUYS

Use unit amounts to decide which is the better value for money.

EXAMPLE

The same brand of coffee is sold in two different sized jars.
Which jar represents the better value for money?

186p   247p

POTS Coffee 100g   POTS Coffee 250g

- Find the cost per gram for both jars.
  100 g costs 186p so 186 ÷ 100 = 1.86p per gram.
  250 g costs 247p so 247 ÷ 250 = 0.988p per gram.
- Since the larger jar costs less per gram it is the better value for money.

RATIOS

- **A ratio is used to compare two or more related quantities.**
- **'Compared to' is replaced with two dots :** For example, **'16 boys compared to 20 girls' can be written as 16 : 20.**
- **To simplify ratios, divide both parts of the ratio by the highest factor. For example,**
  16 : 20 = 4 : 5
  (Divide both sides by 4).

EXAMPLES
- **Simplify the ratio 21 : 28.**
  21 : 28 = 3 : 4 (Divide both sides by 7).
- **The ratio of red flowers to yellow flowers can be written:**
  10 : 4
  $= \frac{10}{2} : \frac{4}{2}$
  = 5 : 2
  In other words, for every 5 red flowers there are 2 yellow flowers.
  To express the ratio 5 : 2 in the ratio n : 1, divide both sides by 2.
  $= \frac{5}{2} : 2$
  = 2.5 : 1

QUICK TEST

1. Write the following ratios in their simplest form:
   a) 12 : 15
   b) 6 : 12
   c) 25 : 10
2. Three sisters share 60 sweets between them in the ratios 2 : 3 : 7. How many sweets does each sister receive?
3. If 15 oranges cost £1.80, how much will 23 identical oranges cost?
4. A map is being enlarged in the ratio 12 : 7. If the road length was 21 cm on the original map, what is the length of the road on the enlarged map?

1. a) 4 : 5 b) 1 : 2 c) 5 : 2   2. 10, 15 and 35 sweets respectively   3. £2.76   4. 36 cm

$$x^a \times x^b = x^{a+b}$$

INDICES

An index is sometimes known as a power.

EXAMPLES

6^4 is read as 6 to the <u>power</u> of <u>4</u>. It means 6 x 6 x 6 x 6.

2^7 is read as 2 to the <u>power</u> <u>7</u>. It means 2 x 2 x 2 x 2 x 2 x 2 x 2.

$$a^b$$

the <u>base</u> ⟶ a^b ⟵ the <u>index</u> or <u>power</u>

The <u>base</u> has to be the <u>same</u> when the rules of indices are applied.

RULES OF INDICES

Indices are a very common topic on the non-calculator paper.

<u>You</u> <u>need</u> <u>to</u> <u>learn</u> <u>these</u> <u>rules</u>:

• When <u>multiplying</u>, <u>add</u> the powers.

$$4^7 \times 4^3 = 4^{7+3} = 4^{10}$$

• When <u>dividing</u>, <u>subtract</u> the powers.

$$6^9 \div 6^4 = 6^{9-4} = 6^5$$

• When <u>raising</u> <u>one</u> <u>power</u> <u>to</u> <u>another</u>, <u>multiply</u> the powers.

$$(7^2)^4 = 7^{2 \times 4} = 7^8$$

• Anything raised to the <u>power</u> <u>zero</u> is just 1, provided the number is not zero.

$$5^0 = 1 \qquad 6^0 = 1$$
$$2.7189^0 = 1 \qquad 0^0 = \text{undefined}$$

• Anything to the <u>power 1</u> is just <u>itself</u>.

$$15^1 = 15 \qquad 1923^1 = 1923$$

The above rules also apply when the powers are negative.

EXAMPLES

$$6^{-2} \times 6^{12} = 6^{-2+12} = 6^{10}$$

$$(6^4)^{-2} = 6^{4 \times -2} = 6^{-8}$$

$$8^{-4} \times 8^{-3} = 8^{-4+-3} = 8^{-7}$$

$$5^0 = 1$$

INDICES AND ALGEBRA

The rules that apply with numbers also apply with letters.

LAWS OF INDICES

$a^n \times a^m = a^{n+m}$

$a^n \div a^m = a^{n-m}$

$(a^n)^m = a^{n \times m}$

$a^0 = 1$

$a^1 = a$

Examiner's Top Tip
Indices are becoming a very common topic on the non-calculator paper — learn the rules and you should be OK!

EXAMPLES

$4\chi^2 \times 3\chi^5 = 12\chi^7$

note that the numbers are multiplied

but the powers of the same letter are added.

$12\chi^4 \div 3\chi^7 = 4\chi^{-3}$

$(7x^2)^2 = 49\chi^4$

$\chi^0 = 1$

$(2\chi^4)^3 = 8\chi^{12}$

simplify
$\dfrac{3\chi^7 \times 4\chi^9}{6\chi^4} = \dfrac{12\chi^{16}}{6\chi^4} = 2\chi^{12}$

work this out in 2 stages

simplify
$\chi^6 \times 4\chi^3 = 4\chi^9$

simplify
$\dfrac{12a^2b^3}{6a^3b^2} = \dfrac{2b}{a}$

simplify
$\dfrac{4a^4b^3}{2ab} = 2a^3b^2$

HIGHER LEVEL OF INDICES

At the higher level there are a few more properties of indices that need to be learnt.

1. NEGATIVE POWERS

These just turn it <u>upside down</u> (or the reciprocal) and make the <u>power positive</u>.

In general $\quad a^{-n} = \dfrac{1}{a^n}$

EXAMPLES

$4^{-2} = \dfrac{1}{4^2} = \dfrac{1}{16}$ $\qquad \left(\dfrac{2}{3}\right)^{-2} = \left(\dfrac{3}{2}\right)^2 = \dfrac{9}{4}$ $\qquad 2\chi^{-3} = \dfrac{2}{\chi^3}$

2. POWERS WITH FRACTIONS

These mean <u>roots!</u>

In general $\quad a^{1/m} = \sqrt[m]{a}$

The power $\dfrac{1}{2}$ means square root $\sqrt{}$

The power $\dfrac{1}{3}$ means cube root $\sqrt[3]{}$

The power $\dfrac{1}{4}$ means fourth root $\sqrt[4]{}$, etc.

EXAMPLES

$25^{1/2} = \sqrt{25} = 5$ $\qquad 8^{1/3} = \sqrt[3]{8} = 2$ $\qquad 81^{1/4} = \sqrt[4]{81} = 3$

Sometimes powers and fractions are put together.

In general $\quad a^{n/m} = \left(\sqrt[m]{a}\right)^n$

EXAMPLES

$8^{2/3} = \left(\sqrt[3]{8}\right)^2 = 2^2 = 4$ $\qquad 64^{5/6} = \left(\sqrt[6]{64}\right)^5 = 2^5 = 32$

If you have a negative number, remember to turn it upside down as well (i.e. take the reciprocal).

$125^{-2/3} = \dfrac{1}{125^{2/3}} = \dfrac{1}{(\sqrt[3]{125})^2} = \dfrac{1}{5^2} = \dfrac{1}{25}$

$(2\chi)^{-3} = \dfrac{1}{(2\chi)^3} = \dfrac{1}{8\chi^3}$

QUICK TEST

1. **Simplify the following:**
   a) $12^4 \times 12^8$ b) $9^{-2} \times 9^{-4}$ c) 4^0
   d) $18^6 \div 18^{-2}$ e) $(4^2)^5$ f) 1^{20}

2. **Simplify the following:**
   a) $\chi^4 \times \chi^9$ b) $2\chi^6 \times 3\chi^7$ c) $12\chi^4 \div 3\chi^2$
   d) $25\chi^9 \div 5\chi^{-2}$ e) $\dfrac{5\chi^6 \times 4\chi^9}{10\chi^3}$

3. **Evaluate:**
   a) $(64)^{2/3}$ b) 5^{-3} c) $144^{1/2}$ d) $36^{-1/2}$

4. **Simplify:**
   a) $(4\chi)^{-2}$ b) $(6\chi^2y^4)^{-2}$

3. a) 16 b) $^1/_{125}$ c) 12 d) $^1/_6$ 4. a) $\dfrac{1}{16\chi^2}$ b) $\dfrac{1}{36\chi^4y^8}$

1. a) 12^{12} b) 9^{-6} c) 1 d) 18^8 e) 4^{10} f) 1   2. a) χ^{13} b) $6\chi^{13}$ c) $4\chi^2$ d) $5\chi^{11}$ e) $2\chi^{12}$

STANDARD INDEX FORM (OR STANDARD FORM)

Standard index form is used to write very large numbers or very small numbers in a simpler way. When written in standard form the number will be written as:

$$a \times 10^n$$

a must be between 1 and 10, $1 \leq a < 10$
The value of n is the number of times the decimal point has to move to the right to return the number to its original value.

Learn these three rules
1) The front number must always be between 1 and 10
2) The power of 10, n, is purely how far the decimal point moves
3) If the number is BIG   If the number is SMALL
   n is positive   n is negative

BIG NUMBERS

EXAMPLES
- Write 6230000 in standard form. Move the decimal point to between the 6 and 2 to give 6.230000 ($1 \leq 6.23 < 10$). Count how many places the decimal point needs to be moved to restore the number.
6 2 3 0 0 0 0   (6 places)
In standard form 6230000 = 6.23×10^6

$4371 = 4.371 \times 10^3$ in standard form.

SMALL NUMBERS

EXAMPLES
- Write 0.00371 in standard form. Move the decimal point to between the 3 and 7 to give 3.71 ($1 \leq 3.71 < 10$). Count how many places the decimal point has been moved.
0.0 0 3 7 1 (3 places)
In standard form $0.00371 = 3.71 \times 10^{-3}$

This means that the decimal point is moved 3 places to the left.

$0.0000479 = 4.79 \times 10^{-5}$ in standard form.

Watch Out!

Several common mistakes when answering standard form questions are:

- Reading a calculator display 2.4⁰⁷ incorrectly and writing down 2.4^7 instead of 2.4×10^7
- Forgetting to write the answer in standard form particularly on the non-calculator paper

e.g. $(2 \times 10^6) \times (6 \times 10^3)$ $= (2 \times 6) \times (10^6 \times 10^3)$

$= 12 \times 10^9$

$= 1.2 \times 10^{10}$

STANDARD FORM AND THE CALCULATOR

To key a number in standard form into the calculator, use the EXP key.
(Some calculators use EE. Make sure that you check your calculator,
as calculators vary greatly.)

EXAMPLES
6.23×10^6 can be keyed in as: 6 . 2 3 EXP 6
4.93×10^{-5} can be keyed in as: 4 . 9 3 EXP 5 $+/-$
Most calculators do not show standard form correctly on the display.
7.632^{09} means 7.632×10^9. 4.62^{-07} means 4.62×10^{-7}.
Remember to put in the x 10 part if it has been left out.

CALCULATIONS WITH STANDARD FORM

Use the calculator to do complex calculations in standard form.
EXAMPLES
$(2.6 \times 10^3) \times (8.9 \times 10^{12}) = 2.314 \times 10^{16}$
This would be keyed in as:

Just key in as normal:
2 . 7 EXP 3 $+/-$

2 . 6 EXP 3 $\times$ 8 . 9 EXP 1 2 $=$

Check that for $(1.8 \times 10^6) \div (2.7 \times 10^{-3})$ the answer is 6.6×10^8
If a calculation with standard form is on the non-calculator paper,
the laws of indices can be used when multiplying and dividing
numbers written in standard form.

EXAMPLES
$(2.4 \times 10^{-4}) \times (3 \times 10^7)$
$= (2.4 \times 3) \times (10^{-4} \times 10^7)$
$= 7.2 \times (10^{-4+7})$
$= 7.2 \times 10^3$

$(12.4 \times 10^{-4}) \div (4 \times 10^7)$
$= (12.4 \div 4) \times (10^{-4} \div 10^7)$
$= 3.1 \times (10^{-4-7})$
$= 3.1 \times 10^{-11}$

Examiner's Top Tip
Standard form questions are very common on both the calculator and non-calculator paper.

QUICK TEST

1. Write the following numbers in standard form:
   a) 630000   b) 2730
   c) 0.0000429   d) 0.00000063

2. Without a calculator work out the following, leaving your answer in standard form.
   a) $(2 \times 10^5) \times (3 \times 10^7)$ b) $(6.1 \times 10^{12}) \times (2 \times 10^{-4})$
   c) $(8 \times 10^9) \div (2 \times 10^6)$ d) $(6 \times 10^8) \div (2 \times 10^{-10})$

3. Work these out on a calculator. Give your answers to 3 s.f.
   a) $\dfrac{1.279 \times 10^9}{2.94 \times 10^{-2}}$ b) $(1.693 \times 10^4) \times (2.71 \times 10^{12})$

4) Calculate, giving your answer in standard form correct to 3 s.f.
   $\dfrac{(3.72 \times 10^8) - (1.6 \times 10^4)}{3.81 \times 10^{-3}}$

4. 9.76×10^{10}
1. a) 6.3×10^5 b) 2.73×10^3 c) 4.29×10^{-5} d) 6.3×10^{-7} 2. a) 6×10^{12} b) 1.22×10^9 c) 4×10^3 d) 3×10^{18} 3. a) 4.35×10^{10} b) 4.59×10^{16}

DIRECT AND INVERSE PROPORTION

The notation $\propto$ means 'is directly proportional to'. This is often abbreviated to 'is proportional to'. For example, $y \propto x^3$ is read as 'y is proportional to x cubed'.

DIRECT PROPORTION

$y \propto x$ means that when x is multiplied by a number, then so is the corresponding value of y.

EXAMPLE

	x2	x3	x4
x	2 → **4** → 12 → 48
y	3 → **6** → 18 → 72
	x2	x3	x4

If $y \propto x^2$, when x is multiplied by a number, y is multiplied by the square of that number.

EXAMPLE

	x2	x3	x4
x	2 → **4** → 12 → 48
y	3 → **12** → 108 → 1728
	$x2^2$	$x3^2$	$x4^2$

For direct proportion, the graph of y against x goes through the origin.
For $y \propto x$, the graph is a straight line through the origin.

A straight line through the origin

INVERSE PROPORTION

$y \propto 1/x$ means that y is inversely proportional to x, when x is multiplied by a number, then y is divided by that number and vice versa.

EXAMPLE

	x4	x3	÷2
x	4 → 16 → 48 → 24
y	12 → 3 → 1 → 2
	÷4	÷3	x2

If $y \propto 1/x^2$, when x is multiplied by a number, y is divided by the square of the number and vice versa.

EXAMPLE

	÷2	x4
x	10 → 5 → 20
y	4 → 16 → 1
	$x2^2$	$÷4^2$

For inverse proportion, the graphs of y against x go to infinity when x or $y = 0$. The graph of $y = \frac{1}{x}$ look like this:

VARIATION

These are common GCSE questions that usually involve statements, such as:

'a is proportional to the square of b'
'c is proportional to the square root of d'
'p is inversely proportional to a^2'
'd varies as the square of x'

EXAMPLE

The value (V) of a diamond varies directly as the square of its weight (w). A diamond weighing 5.0 g is worth £2500. How heavy is a diamond that is worth £6000?

Step 1 Change the sentence into a proportionality using the symbol $\propto$. $V \propto w^2$

Step 2 Replace $\propto$ with = k to make an equation.
  $V = kw^2$

Step 3 Substitute the values given in the question in order to find k. $2500 = k \times 5^2$

Step 4 Rearrange the equation to find the value of k.
  $\frac{2500}{5^2} = k$ ∴ $k = 100$

Step 5 Put the value of k back into the equation.
  $V = 100w^2$

Step 6 Now answer the question using the equation you have found.
  $6000 = 100 \times w^2$
  $\frac{6000}{100} = w^2$
  $w = \sqrt{60}$
  $w = 7.75$ g (2dp)

You use exactly the same steps if y is inversely proportional to x, except the equation in Step 2 would be $y = \frac{k}{x}$.

Examiner's Top Tip
Variation questions are common on higher tier papers and are worth a lot of marks. Learn the steps shown but, above all, read the information carefully and underline key facts because often a cube or a square is missed from the equation.

QUICK TEST

1. y is inversely proportional to the square of x. If $x = 5$ when $y = 4$, work out the value of y when $x = 10$.
2. p varies as the square root of t. If $t = 16$ when $p = 12$, find the value of p when $t = 49$.
3. s is inversely proportional to the cube of r. If $r = 2$ when $s = 5$, what is the value of r when $s = 10$?

3. r = 1.587 (equation s = $\frac{40}{r^3}$)
1. y = 1 (equation y = $\frac{100}{x^2}$)   2. p = 21 (equation p = $3\sqrt{t}$)

RECURRING DECIMALS AND SURDS

CHANGING RECURRING DECIMALS INTO FRACTIONS

As recurring decimals are rational numbers, we can change them to fractions using this method.

EXAMPLE

Change $0.\dot{1}\dot{3}$ to a fraction in its lowest terms.

Let $\chi = 0.131313\ldots(1)$
then $100\chi = 13.131313\ldots(2)$
(Multiply by 10^n, where n is the length of the recurring pattern. In this example it is 2.)

Subtract equation (1) from equation (2)
$99\chi = 13$
This has the effect of making the recurring pattern disappear.

Divide to leave χ
$\chi = \frac{13}{99}$

Since 13 is a prime number, this fraction is in its lowest terms.
so $0.\dot{1}\dot{3} = \frac{13}{99}$

'TRICK' METHOD

There is a quick method of changing recurring decimals to fractions – the fraction has the repeating unit on the top and the same number of nines on the bottom.

EXAMPLES

$0.\dot{2} = \frac{2}{9}$ $0.\dot{4}\dot{1} = \frac{41}{99}$ $0.\dot{1}2\dot{3} = \frac{123}{999}$ $0.\dot{2}71\dot{3} = \frac{2713}{9999}$

Remember to simplify if possible.

If you have a question where there is one or more numbers that are not repeated, extra care is needed.

EXAMPLE

Change $0.2\dot{3}$ into a fraction.
$\chi = 0.2333\ldots(1)$
$10\chi = 2.3333\ldots(2)$ multiply by 10
$100\chi = 23.3333\ldots(3)$ multiply by 100

Subtract equation (2) from equation (3)
$90\chi = 21$
$\chi = \frac{21}{90}$
$\chi = \frac{7}{30}$

SURDS

Numbers written under a square root sign are called surds – $\sqrt{2}$, $\sqrt{3}$, $\sqrt{13}$ etc.

MANIPULATING SURDS

To work with surds there are a few rules to learn.

1. $\sqrt{a} \times \sqrt{b} = \sqrt{ab}$
   example $\sqrt{3} \times \sqrt{5} = \sqrt{15}$

2. $(\sqrt{b})^2 = \sqrt{b} \times \sqrt{b} = b$
   example $(\sqrt{3})^2 = 3$

3. $\frac{\sqrt{a}}{\sqrt{b}} = \sqrt{\frac{a}{b}}$
   example $\frac{\sqrt{10}}{\sqrt{2}} = \sqrt{\frac{10}{2}} = \sqrt{5}$

4. $(a + \sqrt{b})^2 = (a + \sqrt{b})(a + \sqrt{b}) = a^2 + 2a\sqrt{b} + (\sqrt{b})^2 = a^2 + 2a\sqrt{b} + b$

5. $(a + \sqrt{b})(a - \sqrt{b}) = a^2 - a\sqrt{b} + a\sqrt{b} - (\sqrt{b})^2 = a^2 - b$

EXAMPLES

1. **Simplify** $\sqrt{200}$
   (Hint – look for perfect square factors.)
   $\sqrt{200} = \sqrt{2} \times \sqrt{100}$
   $= 10 \times \sqrt{2}$
   $= 10\sqrt{2}$

2. **Simplify** $(\sqrt{2} + 3)(\sqrt{2} + 3)$
   $= (\sqrt{2})^2 + 3\sqrt{2} + 3\sqrt{2} + 9$
   $= 2 + 6\sqrt{2} + 9$
   $= 11 + 6\sqrt{2}$

3. **Simplify** $\frac{1}{\sqrt{5}}$
   multiply the top and bottom by $\sqrt{5}$
   $\frac{1}{\sqrt{5}} \times \frac{\sqrt{5}}{\sqrt{5}}$
   $= \frac{\sqrt{5}}{5}$

   > This is known as rationalising the denominator

Examiner's Top Tip
Practise changing recurring decimals to fractions by using a calculator to check if you are right.

QUICK TEST

1. **Change the following recurring decimals into fractions. Write them in their simplest form.**
   a) $0.\dot{1}\dot{5}$ b) $0.\dot{7}$ c) $0.2\dot{8}\dot{3}$

2. **Simplify the following:**
   a) $\sqrt{75}$ b) $\sqrt{500}$ c) $(\sqrt{2} - 3)^2$ d) $6(\sqrt{2} + 3) - \sqrt{2}(2 + \sqrt{3})$

3. **Simplify** $\frac{1}{\sqrt{3}}$

3. $\frac{\sqrt{3}}{3}$
2. a) $5\sqrt{3}$ b) $10\sqrt{5}$ c) $11 - 6\sqrt{2}$ d) $4\sqrt{2} - \sqrt{6} + 18$
1. a) $\frac{15}{99} = \frac{5}{33}$ b) $\frac{7}{9}$ c) $\frac{281}{990}$

27

UPPER AND LOWER BOUNDS OF MEASUREMENT

FINDING THE MAXIMUM AND MINIMUM POSSIBLE VALUES OF A CALCULATION

When calculations are carried out using rounded off values, then the calculated value can lie between a maximum and a minimum possible value.

EXAMPLE 1

A desk measures 62 cm by 95 cm. Work out the lower and upper bounds of the area of the desk.

lower bound

94.5
61.5

upper bound

95.5
62.5

lower bound of area
$= 61.5 \times 94.5 = 5811.75$ cm^2

The rounded value $= 95 \times 62 = 5890$ cm^2

upper bound of area
62.5×95.5

5968.75 cm^2

EXAMPLE 2

A toy has a mass of 120 g and a volume of 60 cm^3, both measurements are correct to the nearest 10 units.
Calculate the lower and upper bounds for the density of the toy.

the upper and lower bounds of the mass are: 115 g and 125 g

the upper and lower bounds of the volume are: 55 cm^3 and 65 cm^3.

lower bound of density $= \dfrac{115}{65} = 1.77$ g/cm^3 (2dp)

upper bound of density $= \dfrac{125}{55} = 2.27$ g/cm^3 (2dp)

When working out the lower and upper bounds in multiplication and addition, it is quite straight forward. For subtraction and division more care is needed.

Here are a few tips:

1. **Finding a difference**

upper bound $=$ upper bound of larger quantity $-$ lower bound of smaller quantity

lower bound $=$ lower bound of larger quantity $-$ upper bound of smaller quantity

2. **Division**

upper bound $= \dfrac{\text{upper bound of quantity 1}}{\text{lower bound of quantity 2}}$

lower bound $= \dfrac{\text{lower bound of quantity 1}}{\text{upper bound of quantity 2}}$

MAXIMUM PERCENTAGE ERROR

This is found by using the following formula:

$$\text{Percentage error} = \frac{\text{maximum error}}{\text{original}} \times 100\%$$

The 'original' is the value that is the furthest from the rounded value.

For the desk in the previous example: Percentage error

$$= \frac{5968.75 - 5890}{5968.75} \times 100\% = 1.32\%$$

Calculations are not always as straightforward as this.

UPPER AND LOWER BOUNDS FOR A SINGLE MEASUREMENT

If a length X(cm) is given as 6.2, correct to the nearest millimetre, then using the usual conventions of rounding

$$6.15 \leq X < 6.25$$

6.15 is called
the <u>lower</u> bound

6.25 is called
the <u>upper</u> bound

In general, the real value can be as much as half the rounded unit above and below the rounded off value.

EXAMPLES

If $X = 6.23$ (correct to 2dp) then the rounded unit is 0.01, so the real value can be anything between
$$6.225 \leq 6.23 < 6.235$$

Examiner's Top Tip
This is a popular topic on exam papers. You must be careful on questions with division and subtraction, as it is easy to make a mistake. If in doubt, try all the different combinations (if you have time), but don't forget to cross out the ones you don't want!

QUICK TEST

1. If $X = \frac{4}{y}$ and y = 6.2 (1dp), calculate the upper and lower bounds of X.

2. If h = ab, a = 2.7 (1dp) and b = 20 (nearest whole number), calculate the lower and upper bounds of h.

1. upper bound = 0.65 (2dp)   lower bound = 0.64
∴ $0.64 \leq X < 0.65$

2. upper bound = 56.375   lower bound = 51.675
$51.675 \leq X < 56.375$

EXAM QUESTIONS - Use the questions to test your progress. Check your answers on page 110.

1. Mrs Patel inherits £55 000. She divides the money between her children in the ratio 3 : 3 : 5.
How much does the child with the largest share receive?

....

(c) 2. Work these out on your calculator, giving your answers to 3 s.f.
a) $\dfrac{4.2\,(3.6 + 5.1)}{2 - 1.9}$ =   b) $\dfrac{3.8 + 4.6}{2.9 \times 4.1}$ =

....

....

3. Show how you would estimate the answer to this expression without using a calculator.
Work out the estimate.
$$\frac{8.7 + 9.02}{0.2 \times 48}$$

....

....

(c) 4. Toothpaste is sold in three different sized tubes.
      50 ml = £1.24   75 ml = £1.96   100 ml = £2.42
Which of the tubes of toothpaste is the best value for money?
You must show full working out in order to justify your answer.

....

....

5. A piece of writing paper is 0.01 cm thick. A notepad has 150 sheets of paper.
How thick is the notepad?

....

(c) 6. The price of a CD player has been reduced by 15% in a sale. It now costs £320.
What was the original price?

....

(c) 7. A car was bought in 1997 for £9000. Each year it depreciates in value by 15%.
What is the car worth two years later?

....

(c) 8. James put £632 in a new savings account. At the end of every year interest at 4.2% is added to the amount
in his savings account at the beginning of that year.
Calculate the amount in James's savings account at the end of 3 years.

....

9. The price of a television has risen from £350 to £420.
Work out the percentage increase in the price.

....

(c) 10. Write these numbers in standard form:
a) 2 670 000   b) 4270   c) 0.03296   d) 0.027

....

(c) Indicates that a calculator may be used

11. The mass of a hair is 0.000042 g.
a) Write this number in standard form ....
b) Calculate, in standard form, the mass of 6×10^5 hairs ....

12. Work out the answers to these questions giving your answer in standard form:
a) $(2 \times 10^9) \times (6 \times 10^{12})$ ....
b) $(8 \times 10^9) \div (4 \times 10^{-2})$ ....

(C) 13. y is directly proportional to x. When $x = 4$ $y = 12$. Find:
a) an equation connecting x and y
b) the value of x when $y = 20$.

....
....

(C) 14. y is inversely proportional to x^2. When $x = 2$ $y = 5$. Find:
a) the value of y when $x = 4$
b) the value of x when $y = 10$.

....
....

15. Write these recurring decimals as fractions:
a) $0.\dot{4}$ b) $0.\dot{2}\dot{1}$ c) $0.\dot{2}3\dot{4}$ d) $0.2\dot{7}$

....

16. Simplify the following:
a) $\sqrt{12}$ b) $\sqrt{75}$ c) $\sqrt{200}$ d) $\sqrt{6}(\sqrt{3} - 2)$ e) $\sqrt{3} \times \sqrt{75}$

....

(C) 17. A rectangular carpet is measured as 1.42 m by 1.61 m. Find the upper and the lower bounds for the area of the carpet.

....

(C) 18. Thomas cycles 1250 m in 95 s. Assuming that the time is measured to the nearest second and the distance to the nearest 10 metres, find the upper and lower bounds of Thomas' average speed in metres per second.

....

(C) 19. The area of a circle is 142 cm² (correct to 3 significant figures).
Find the upper and lower bounds of the radius of the circle.

....

20. Evaluate the following:
a) $64^{\frac{1}{3}}$ b) $8^{\frac{2}{3}}$ c) 6^{-2} d) $49^{\frac{1}{2}}$ e) $25^{-\frac{1}{2}}$ f) $(4)^{-2}$ g) $\left(\frac{5}{7}\right)^{-2}$

....
....

How did you do?

1–5	correct	....start again
6–10	correct	....getting there
11–15	correct	....good work
16–20	correct	....excellent

ALGEBRA ①

THIS INVOLVES USING LETTERS

ALGEBRAIC CONVENTIONS

- A <u>term</u> is a collection of numbers, letters and brackets, all multiplied together.
- Terms are separated by + and – signs. Each term has a + or – <u>attached</u> <u>to the</u> <u>front</u> <u>of it</u>.

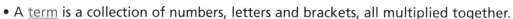

$$3xy - 5r - 2x^2 + 4$$

invisible + sign   xy term   r term x^2 term   number term

- 3 x a is written without the multiplication sign as 3a.
  a + a + a = 3a
  a x a x a = a^3, not 3a
  a x a x 2 = $2a^2$, not $(2a)^2$
  a x b x 2 = 2ab

COLLECTING LIKE TERMS

Expressions can be simplified by collecting <u>like terms</u>.
Only collect the terms if their letters and powers are <u>identical</u>.

Add the a terms together, then the terms with b. Remember a means 1a.

EXAMPLES

$4a + 2a = 6a$

$3a^2 + 6a^2 - 4a^2 = 5a^2$

$4a + 6b - 3a + 2b = a + 8b$

$9a + 4b$ cannot be simplified since there are no like terms.

$3xy + 2yx = 5xy$

Remember xy means the same as yx

WRITING FORMULAE

Quite often in the exam you are asked to write a formula when given some information or a diagram.

EXAMPLE
Frances buys x books at £2.50 each. She pays with a £20 note. If she receives C pounds change write down as a formula.

this represents the amount of money spent on books

$$C = 20 - 2.50x$$

notice that no £ signs are put in our formula

this is the amount of money she spent

If in doubt check by substituting a value for x i.e: if she bought 1 book x = 1 so her change would be 20 – 2.50 x 1 = £17.50

EXAMPLE
Some patterns are made by using grey and white paving slabs.

Write a formula for the number of grey paving slabs (g) in a pattern that uses (w) white ones.

Formula is g = 2w + 2
2w represents the 2 layers, + 2 gives the grey slabs which are on either end of the white ones.

FORMULAE, EXPRESSIONS AND SUBSTITUTING

p + 3 is an <u>expression</u>.

y = p + 3 is a <u>formula</u>. The value of y depends on the value of p.

<u>Replacing</u> a <u>letter</u> with <u>a</u> <u>number</u> is <u>called</u> substitution. When substituting:

- Write out the expression first and then replace the letters with the values given.
- Work out the value on your calculator. Use bracket keys where possible and pay attention to the order of operations.

Try these out on your calculator

EXAMPLES

Using W = 5.6, t = –7.1 and u = $\frac{2}{5}$, find the value of these expressions, giving your answers to 3 s.f.

a) $\frac{W + t}{u}$ b) $W - \frac{t}{u}$ c) $\sqrt{Wt^2}$

Remember to show the substitution.

a) $\frac{W + t}{u} = \frac{5.6 + (-7.1)}{\frac{2}{5}} = -3.75$

b) $W - \frac{t}{u} = 5.6 - \frac{(-7.1)}{\frac{2}{5}} = 23.4$

You may need to treat t² as (-7.1)², depending on your calculator.

c) $\sqrt{Wt^2} = \sqrt{5.6 \times (-7.1)^2} = 16.8$

Examiner's Top Tip
When substituting into an expression or formula you must show each step in your working out. By showing your substitution you will obtain method marks even if you get the final answer wrong.

USING FORMULAE

A formula describes the relationship between two (or more) variables.
A formula must have an = sign in it.

EXAMPLE

Andrew hires a van. There is a standing charge of £8 and then it costs £3 per hour. How much does it cost for:

a) 6 hours' drive
b) y hours' drive
c) Write a formula for the total hire cost C.

This is a formula which works out the cost of hiring the van for any number of hours.

a) $8 + (3 \times 6) = £26$
b) $8 + (3 \times y) = 8 + 3y$
d) $C = 8 + 3y$

QUICK TEST

1. Simplify these expressions by collecting like terms:

   a) 5a + 2a + 3a

   b) 6a – 3b + 4b + 2a

   c) 5x – 3x + 7x – 2y + 6y

   d) $3xy^2 - 2x^2y + 6x^2y - 8xy^2$

2. Using p = 6.2, r = –3.2 and s = $\frac{2}{3}$, find the value of these expressions, giving your answer to 3 s.f. Use a calculator.

   a) pr + s

   b) $p^2s - r$

   c) $r^2 - p/s$

   d) $(ps - r)^2$

1. a) 10a b) 8a + b c) 9x + 4y d) $4x^2y - 5xy^2$ 2. a) –19.2 b) 28.8 c) 0.940 d) 53.8

MULTIPLYING OUT BRACKETS

The subject of the formula is usually written first.

- This helps to simplify algebraic expressions.
- The term **outside** the brackets **multiplies** **each** **separate term** **inside** **the brackets**.

EXAMPLES

$3(2x + 5) = 6x + 15$ $(3 \times 2x = 6x, 3 \times 5 = 15)$

$a(3a - 4) = 3a^2 - 4a$ $b(2a + 3b - c) = 2ab + 3b^2 - bc$

If the term outside the bracket is **negative**, all of the signs of the terms inside the bracket are **changed** when multiplying out.

EXAMPLES

$-4(2x + 3) = -8x - 12$ $-2(4 - 3x) = -8 + 6x$

To simplify expressions expand the brackets first then collect like terms.

EXAMPLES

Expand and simplify $2(x - 3) + x(x + 4)$.

$2(x - 3) + x(x + 4)$

$= 2x - 6 + x^2 + 4x$ Multiply out the brackets.

$= x^2 + 6x - 6$ Collect like terms.

Examiner's Top Tip
If you are asked to <u>expand</u> brackets it just means multiply them out. When you have finished multiplying out the brackets <u>simplify</u> by collecting like terms in order to pick up the final mark.

MULTIPLICATION OF TWO BRACKETS

Each term in the first bracket is multiplied with each term in the second bracket.

Each term in the first bracket is multiplied with the second; simplify by collecting like terms.

EXAMPLES

Expand and simplify the following.

a) $(x + 2)(x + 3)$ $= x(x + 3) + 2(x + 3)$
$= x^2 + 3x + 2x + 6$
$= x^2 + 5x + 6$

b) $(2x + 4)(3x - 2) = 2x(3x - 2) + 4(3x - 2)$
$= 6x^2 - 4x + 12x - 8$
$= 6x^2 + 8x - 8$

c) $(x + y)^2$ $= x(x + y) + y(x + y)$
$= x^2 + xy + xy + y^2$
$= x^2 + 2xy + y^2$

A common error is to think that $(a + b)^2$ means $a^2 + b^2$

(this is an identity; it is true for all values of x).

REARRANGING FORMULAE

The <u>subject</u> of a formula is the letter that appears on its own on one side of the formula.

EXAMPLES

Make p the subject of these formulae:

a) $r = (p + 6)^2$ b) $y = \dfrac{p + r}{6}$

a) $r = (p + 6)^2$ Deal with the power first. Take the square root of both sides.

$\sqrt{r} = p + 6$ Remove any terms added or subtracted.
So subtract 6 from both sides.

$\sqrt{r} - 6 = p$ <u>or</u> $p = \sqrt{r} - 6$

(b) $y = \dfrac{p + r}{6}$ Deal with the term dividing p; multiply both sides by 6.

$6y = p + r$ Remove r by subtracting r from both sides.

$6y - r = p$ <u>or</u> $p = 6y - r$

FACTORISATION (PUTTING BRACKETS IN)

This is the reverse of expanding brackets. An expression is put into brackets by taking out <u>common</u> <u>factors</u>.

ONE BRACKET

$$y(x + 4) \xrightarrow{\text{expand}} xy + 4y$$
$$\xleftarrow{\text{factorise}}$$

To <u>factorise</u> $xy + 4y$:
• recognise that y is a factor of each term;
• take out the common factor;

• the expression is completed inside the bracket, so that the result is equivalent to $xy + 4y$, when multiplied out.

EXAMPLES
Factorise the following.
(a) $5x^2 + x = x(5x + 1)$
(b) $4x^2 + 8x = 4x(x + 2)$
(c) $5x^3 + 15x^4 = 5x^3(1 + 3x)$

Factorising can be useful when simplifying algebraic fractions.

EXAMPLE
Simplify $\dfrac{5x + 15}{x + 3} = \dfrac{5\cancel{(x + 3)}}{\cancel{(x + 3)}} = 5$

$a = b^2$ $v^2 = 5^3 \times 5a$

$2(x - 3)$

ALGEBRA ②

$x = y^2$

$\dfrac{r = p^2}{q}$

$2(3 + x - 1)$ $3(y + x - 3)$

FACTORISATION OF A QUADRATIC

TWO BRACKETS
Two brackets are obtained when a quadratic expression of the type $x^2 + bx + c$ is factorised.

These multiply to give 2, and add to give 3 in $3x$

$$(x + 2)(x + 1) \xrightarrow{\text{expand}} x^2 + 3x + 2$$
$$\xleftarrow{\text{factorise}}$$

EXAMPLES
Factorise the following.
a) $x^2 + 5x - 6 = (x - 1)(x + 6)$
b) $x^2 - 6x + 8 = (x - 2)(x - 4)$
c) $x^2 - 25 = (x - 5)(x + 5)$

this is known as the difference of two squares. In general $x^2 - a^2 = (x - a)(x + a)$.

QUICK TEST

1. Multiply out the brackets and simplify where possible:

   a) $3(x + 2)$ b) $2(x + y)$

   c) $-3(2x + 4)$ d) $(x + 2)(x + 3)$

   e) $(y - 4)(y - 3)$ f) $(a + 2)^2$

2. Factorise the following expressions:

   a) $3x + 6$ b) $5y - 15$

   c) $12x^2 - 6x$ d) $x^2 - 5x - 6$

   e) $x^2 - 3x + 2$ f) $x^2 - 16$

3. Make u the subject of the formula $v^2 = u^2 + 2as$.

f) $(x-4)(x+4)$ 3. $u = \pm\sqrt{v^2 - 2as}$

1. a) $3x + 6$ b) $2x + 2y$ c) $-6x - 12$ d) $x^2 + 5x + 6$ e) $y^2 - 7y + 12$ f) $a^2 + 4a + 4$ 2. a) $3(x+2)$ b) $5(y-3)$ c) $6x(2x-1)$ d) $(x-6)(x+1)$ e) $(x-1)(x-2)$

SOLVING EQUATIONS INVOLVING INDICES

Equations sometimes involve indices. You will need to remember the laws of indices to be able to solve them.

EXAMPLE

1 Solve.

$$y^k = \sqrt{y} \div \frac{1}{y^4}$$

$$y^k = y^{1/2} \div y^{-4}$$

$$y^k = y^{1/2 - (-4)}$$

$$y^k = y^{4^{1/2}} \quad \text{comparing indices gives}$$

$$k = 4\tfrac{1}{2}$$

2 Solve.

$$4^{k+1} = 16$$

$$4^{k+1} = 4^2$$

$$k + 1 = 2 \quad \text{rewrite so that the}$$
$$\qquad\qquad\quad \text{bases are the same.}$$

$$k = 1$$

EQUATIONS ①

AN EQUATION INVOLVES AN <u>UNKNOWN</u> VALUE WHICH HAS TO BE WORKED OUT

SOLVING LINEAR EQUATIONS OF THE FORM $a\chi + b = c\chi + d$

The trick with this type of equation is to get the χ's together on one side of the equal sign and the numbers on the other side.

EXAMPLE

Solve:
$$5\chi - 9 = 12 - 4\chi$$
$$9\chi - 9 = 12 \qquad \text{add } 4\chi \text{ to both sides.}$$
$$9\chi = 21 \qquad \text{Add 9 to both sides.}$$
$$\chi = \tfrac{21}{9} = 2\tfrac{1}{3} \qquad \text{If in the exam you do not know that } \tfrac{21}{9} = 2\tfrac{1}{3},$$
$$\qquad\qquad\qquad \text{leave it as } \tfrac{21}{9} \text{ to obtain full marks!}$$

SOLVING QUADRATIC EQUATIONS

Make sure the quadratic equation is equal to zero. Then factorise the quadratic equation.

EXAMPLES

Solve the following:

a) $\chi^2 - 5\chi = 0$ χ is a common factor.

   $\chi(\chi - 5) = 0$

   Either $\chi = 0$ or $\chi - 5 = 0$, i.e. $\chi = 5$

b) $\chi^2 - 3\chi = 10$

   $\chi^2 - 3\chi - 10 = 0$ Make it equal to zero and factorise.

   $(\chi + 2)(\chi - 5) = 0$

   Either $(\chi + 2) = 0$, i.e. $\chi = -2$, or $(\chi - 5) = 0$, i.e. $\chi = 5$

SOLVING LINEAR EQUATIONS WITH BRACKETS

Just because an equation has brackets don't be put off. It's just the same as the other equations once the brackets have been multiplied out.

EXAMPLES

a) Solve:

$$3(x - 2) = 2(x + 6)$$
$$3x - 6 = 2x + 12$$ Multiply out the brackets first.
$$x - 6 = 12$$
$$x = 18$$

b) Solve:

$$5(x - 2) + 6 = 3(x - 4) + 10$$
$$5x - 10 + 6 = 3x - 12 + 10$$
$$5x - 4 = 3x - 2$$
$$2x = 2$$
$$x = 1$$

USING EQUATIONS TO SOLVE PROBLEMS

EXAMPLE

The perimeter of the triangle is 20 cm. Work out the value of x and hence find the length of the 3 sides.

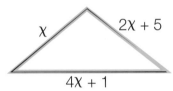

$x + 2x + 5 + 4x + 1 = 20$

$7x + 6 = 20$
$7x = 20 - 6$
$7x = 14$
$x = \frac{14}{7}$
$x = 2$

The perimeter is found by adding lengths together. Collect like terms. Solve the equation as before.

So the lengths of the sides are 2 (= x), 9 (= 4x + 1) and 9 (= 2x + 5)

QUICK TEST

Solve the following equations:

1. $2x - 3 = 9$

2. $4x + 2 = 20$

3. $5x + 3 = 2x + 9$

4. $6x - 1 = 15 + 2x$

5. $3(x + 2) = x + 4$

6. $2(x - 1) = 6(2x + 2)$

7. $x^2 + 4x - 5 = 0$

8. $x^2 - 5x + 6 = 0$

9. $4^{2k - 1} = 32$

1. $x = 6$ 2. $x = 4.5$ 3. $x = 2$ 4. $x = 4$ 5. $x = -1$ 6. $x = -1.4$ 7. $x = 1, x = -5$ 8. $x = 2, x = 3$ 9. $k = 1\frac{3}{4}$

SIMULTANEOUS EQUATIONS

Two equations with two unknowns are called <u>simultaneous equations</u>.
They can be solved in several ways. Solving equations simultaneously involves finding values for the letters that will make both equations work.

GRAPHICAL METHOD

The points at which any two graphs intersect represent the simultaneous solutions of these equations.

EXAMPLE

Solve the simultaneous equations $y = 2x - 1$, $x + y = 5$
• Draw the two graphs.

$y = 2x - 1$ If $x = 0$, $y = -1$
                        If $y = 0$, $x = \frac{1}{2}$
$x + y = 5$ If $x = 0$, $y = 5$
                        If $x = 5$, $y = 0$
• At the point of intersection $x = 2$ and $y = 3$.

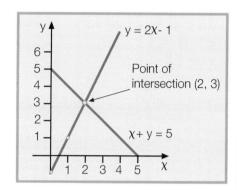

Point of intersection (2, 3)

ELIMINATION METHOD

If the coefficient of one of the letters is the same in both equations, then that letter may be eliminated by subtracting the equations.

EXAMPLE

Solve simultaneously
$$2x + 3y = 6$$
$$x + y = 1$$

STEP 1
Label the equations ① and ②.
$$2x + 3y = 6 \quad ①$$
$$x + y = 1 \quad ②$$

STEP 2
Since no coefficients match multiply equation ② by 2. Rename it equation ③.
$$2x + 3y = 6 \quad ①$$
$$2x + 2y = 2 \quad ③$$

STEP 3
The coefficient of x in equations ① and ③ are the same.
Subtract equation ③ from equation ① and then solve the remaining equation.
$$0x + y = 4$$
$$\therefore y = 4$$

STEP 4
Substitute the value of $y = 4$ into equation ① or equation ②. Solve this equation to find x.
$$x + 4 = 1$$
$$x = 1 - 4$$
$$x = -3$$

STEP 5
Check in equation ①
$$(2 \times -3) + (3 \times 4) = 6$$

The solution is $x = -3$, $y = 4$

Examiner's Top Tip
Simultaneous equations are usually a difficult topic to master. Try to learn the steps outlined above and practise lots of examples. Use the check at the end to make sure that you have the correct answers.

**Remember: To eliminate terms with opposite signs, add the equations
To eliminate terms with the same signs, subtract the equations.**

SOLVING CUBIC EQUATIONS BY TRIAL AND IMPROVEMENT

Trial and improvement gives an approximate solution to equations.

EXAMPLE
The equation $x^3 - 5x = 10$ has a solution between 2 and 3. Find this solution to 2 decimal places.

Draw a table to help.
Substitute different values of x into $x^3 - 5x$.

Examiner's Top Tip
Make sure you write down the solution of x, not the answer to $x^3 - 5x$.

x	$x^3 - 5x$	Comment
2.5	3.125	too small
2.8	7.952	too small
2.9	9.889	too small
2.95	10.922375	too big
2.94	10.712184	too big
2.91	10.092171	too big

At this stage the solution is trapped between 2.90 and 2.91. Checking the middle value $x = 2.905$ gives $x^3 - 5x = 9.99036 \ldots$ which is too small.

2.90	2.905	2.91
(too small)	(too small)	(too big)

The diagram makes it clear that the solution is 2.91 correct to 2 decimal places.

EQUATIONS ②

QUICK TEST

1. Solve the following pairs of simultaneous equations:

   a) $4x + 7y = 10$
      $2x + 3y = 3$

   b) $3a - 5b = 1$
      $2a + 3b = 7$

2. The diagram shows the graphs of the equations $x + y = 2$ and $y = x - 4$.

   Use the diagram to solve the simultaneous equations.

   $x + y = 2$

   $y = x - 4$

3. The equation $y^3 + y = 40$ has a solution between 3 and 4.

   Find this solution to 1 d.p. by using a method of trial and improvement.

1. a) $x = -4.5, y = 4$ b) $a = 2, b = 1$ 2. $x = 3, y = -1$ 3. 3.3

QUADRATIC EQUATIONS

We have already seen how to factorise a quadratic equation of the form $x^2 + bx + c = 0$. Unfortunately, they are not all as easy as this, and so there are several other methods for solving quadratic equations of the form $ax^2 + bx + c = 0$.

1 FACTORISATION

EXAMPLE: Solve $3x^2 - x - 4 = 0$

a) Write out the two brackets and put an x and a $3x$ in each one, since $x \times 3x = 3x^2$.

b) We now need two numbers that multiply to give -4 (one positive and one negative) and, when multiplied by the x terms, add up to $-1x$.

$(3x + 4)(x - 1)$	$4 x -1 = -4$ ✓	$3x \times -1 + 4x = -3x + 4x = x$ incorrect
$(3x - 4)(x + 1)$	$-4 \times 1 = -4$ ✓	$3x \times 1 + -4x = 3x - 4x = -x$ correct

A quick check gives

$(3x - 4)(x + 1) = 3x^2 - x - 4$

the $3x$ and 1 must be in opposite brackets

c) Now solve the equation $(3x - 4)(x + 1) = 0$
Do separately, putting each bracket equal to 0.

$(3x - 4) = 0$ so $x = \frac{4}{3}$ or $(x + 1) = 0$ so $x = -1$

2 THE QUADRATIC FORMULA

The formula can be used to solve any quadratic equation. Only use this equation, though, if the quadratic equation cannot be factorised.

$$x = \frac{-b \pm \sqrt{b^2 - 4ac}}{2a}$$

for any quadratic equation written in the form $ax^2 + bx + c = 0$

EXAMPLE: Find the solutions of $2x^2 + x = 7$ to 2 decimal places.

a) Put the equation into the form $ax^2 + bx + c = 0$: $2x^2 + x - 7 = 0$
b) Identify the values of a, b and c: $a = 2, b = 1, c = -7$
c) Substitute these values into the quadratic formula:

$$x = \frac{-b \pm \sqrt{b^2 - 4ac}}{2a}$$

$$x = \frac{-1 \pm \sqrt{1^2 - (4 \times 2 \times -7)}}{2 \times 2}$$

$$x = \frac{-1 \pm \sqrt{1 + 56}}{4}$$

$$x = \frac{-1 \pm \sqrt{57}}{4}$$

$$x = \frac{-1 - \sqrt{57}}{4}$$

one solution is when we use $-\sqrt{57}$

$$x = \frac{-1 + \sqrt{57}}{4}$$

the other solution is when we use $+\sqrt{57}$

$x = -2.14$ $x = 1.64$

d) To check, put these values into the original equation.
$2 \times (-2.14)^2 + (-2.14) = 7$ ✓
$2 \times (1.64)^2 + (1.64) = 7$ ✓

3 COMPLETING THE SQUARE

This is when quadratic equations are expressed in the form $(x + a)^2 + b = 0$.

EXAMPLE: *Express* $x^2 - 4x + 1 = 0$ *as a completed square and hence solve it.*

a) *Rearrange the equation in the form* $ax^2 + bx + c = 0$. *If 'a' is not 1, then divide the whole equation by a.*
b) *Write the equation in the form* $(x + \frac{b}{2})^2$. *Notice that the number in the bracket is always half the value of b!*
c) *Multiply out the brackets, compare to the original and adjust by adding or subtracting an extra amount.*

1) So	$x^2 - 4x + 1 = 0$	*this is already in the form* $ax^2 + bx + c = 0$ *and a = 1*
2)	$(x - 2)^2$	*half of -4 is -2*
3)	$(x - 2)^2 = x^2 - 4x + 4$	*Multiply out the brackets and now compare to the original* $x^2 - 4x + 1$. *To make* $x^2 - 4x + 4$ *like the original we need to subtract 3.*
	$(x - 2)^2 - 3 = 0$	
4)	$(x - 2)^2 - 3 = 0$	*Now we need to solve the equation.*
	$(x - 2)^2 = 3$	
	$(x - 2) = \pm \sqrt{3}$	$\therefore x = \sqrt{3} + 2$ or $x = -\sqrt{3} + 2$
		$x = 3.73$ $x = 0.27$

FURTHER ALGEBRA AND EQUATIONS

ALGEBRAIC FRACTIONS

When working with algebraic fractions, the rules are the same as for ordinary fractions.

EXAMPLE

a) Addition and subtraction

$$\frac{x+2}{x-1} + \frac{3}{x} = \frac{(x+2)x}{x(x-1)} + \frac{3(x-1)}{x(x-1)} =$$

$$\frac{x^2+2x+3x-3}{x(x-1)} = \frac{x^2+5x-3}{x(x-1)}$$

Always find a common denominator (the same bottom line) and then adjust the numerators. Simplify by multiplying out the numerator and collecting like terms.

b) Multiplication
Simply multiply the numerators together and the denominators together and cancel if possible.

e.g. $\frac{3p^2q}{r^2s} \times \frac{2rs}{9pq^2} = \frac{6p^2qrs}{9pq^2r^2s} = \frac{2p}{3qr}$

c) Division
Remember to turn the second fraction upside down (i.e. take the reciprocal), then multiply and cancel if possible.

e.g. $\frac{6(x+2)}{(x-1)} \div \frac{12(x+2)(x+3)}{(x+1)}$

$$= \frac{\cancel{6(x+2)}}{(x-1)} \times 2\frac{(x+1)}{\cancel{12(x+2)(x+3)}}$$

$$= \frac{(x+1)}{2(x-1)(x+3)}$$

REARRANGING FORMULAE

WHEN THE SUBJECT APPEARS IN MORE THAN ONE TERM

EXAMPLE
Make y the subject of the formula $a = \dfrac{y+b}{y-c}$

$a = \dfrac{y+b}{y-c}$ *multiply both sides by (y − c)*

$a(y-c) = y+b$ *multiply out the brackets*

$ay - ac = y + b$ *collect the terms involving y on one side of the equation*

$ay - y = b + ac$

$y(a-1) = b + ac$ *factorise*

$$y = \frac{(b+ac)}{(a-1)}$$

Examiner's Top Tip
All the techniques outlined in this section are very important! Practise plenty of questions on these topics to help you become confident when working with more complex algebra. GCSE questions on these topics usually carry a lot of marks.

QUICK TEST

1. Solve the following quadratic equations by a) factorisation b) quadratic formula and c) completing the square.

   a) $3x^2 - 7x + 2 = 0$ b) $2x^2 + 5x + 2 = 0$ c) $4x^2 - 7x - 2 = 0$

2. Make r the subject of the formula $p = \dfrac{r-y}{r+s}$

3. Simplify the following algebraic fractions:

   a) $\dfrac{2}{(x+2)} + \dfrac{3}{(x-1)}$ b) $\dfrac{4(s-1)}{3(s+2)} \times \dfrac{(s+2)^2}{8(s-3)}$ c) $\dfrac{8(a^2-b^2)}{3(a+2)} \div \dfrac{4(a-b)}{27(a+1)}$

ALGEBRA

INEQUALITIES

THE 4 INEQUALITY SYMBOLS

> means 'greater than'   ≥ means 'greater than or equal to'
< means 'less than'   ≤ means 'less than or equal to'
So $x > 3$ and $3 < x$ both say 'x is greater than 3'

Inequalities are solved in a similar way to equations. Multiplying and dividing by <u>negative</u> <u>numbers</u> changes the <u>direction</u> of the sign. For example if $-x \geq 5$ then $x \leq -5$.

EXAMPLES

Solve the following inequalities:

a) $4x - 2 < 2x + 6$
$\quad 2x - 2 < 6$ Subtract $2x$ from both sides.
$\quad 2x < 8$ Add 2 to both sides.
$\quad x < 4$ Divide both sides by 2.

The solution of the inequality may be represented on a number line.

$\qquad\qquad\qquad\qquad 4$

Use • when the end point is included and ○ when the end point is not included.

b) $-5 < 3x + 1 \leq 13$ Subtract 1 from each part.
$\quad -6 < 3x \leq 12$ Divide by 3.
$\quad -2 < x \leq 4$

The <u>integer values</u> which satisfy the above inequality are

$$-1, 0, 1, 2, 3, 4.$$

GRAPHS OF INEQUALITIES

The graph of an equation such as $y = 3$ is a line, whereas the graph of the inequality $y < 3$ is a region which has the line $y = 3$ as its <u>boundary</u>.

<u>To</u> <u>show</u> <u>the</u> <u>region</u> <u>for</u> <u>given</u> <u>inequalities</u>:

• Draw the boundary lines first.

• For <u>strict</u> inequalities > and <, the boundary line is not included and is shown as a dotted line.

• It is often easier with several inequalities to shade out the unwanted regions, so that the solution is shown <u>unshaded</u>.

EXAMPLE

The diagram shows unshaded the region $x > 1$, $x + y \leq 4$, $y \geq 0$

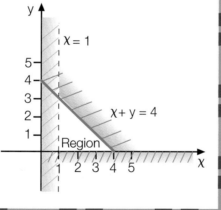

Examiner's Top Tip
Inequalities are solved in a similar way to equations.

QUICK TEST

Solve the following inequalities:

1. $2x - 3 < 9$

2. $5x + 1 \geq 21$

3. $1 \leq 3x - 2 \leq 7$

4. $1 \leq 5x + 2 < 12$

1. $x < 6$ 2. $x \geq 4$ 3. $1 \leq x \leq 3$ 4. $-\frac{1}{5} \leq x < 2$

NUMBER PATTERNS AND SEQUENCES

Examiner's Top Tip
Check your rule for the nth term works, by substituting another value of n into your expression.

A <u>sequence</u> is a list of numbers. There is usually a relationship between the numbers. Each value in the list is called a <u>term</u>.

EXAMPLE
The odd numbers form a sequence 1, 3, 5, 7, 9, 11, . . . in which the terms have a <u>common</u> <u>difference</u> of 2.

IMPORTANT NUMBER SEQUENCES
Square numbers	1, 4, 9, 16, 25, . . .
Cube numbers	1, 8, 27, 64, 125, . . .
Triangular numbers	1, 3, 6, 10, 15, . . .
The Fibonacci sequence	1, 1, 2, 3, 5, 8, 13, . . .

The common difference is 2

FINDING THE NTH TERM OF A LINEAR SEQUENCE

The nth term is often denoted by U_n. For example, the 12th term is U_{12}.
For a linear sequence, the nth term takes the form
$U_n = an + b$.

EXAMPLE
For the sequence of odd numbers, find an expression for the nth term.
1, 3, 5, 7, 9, . . .

- Find the common difference; this is a.
  So a = 2 here. So $U_n = 2n + b$.
- Now substitute the values of U_1 and n.
  n = 1 and $U_1 = 1$.
  This gives 1 = 2 + b.
  So b = –1.
- nth term: $U_n = 2n – 1$.
- Check: for the 10th term $U_{10} = 2 \times 10 – 1 = 19$.

THE NTH TERM OF QUADRATIC SEQUENCE

For a quadratic sequence the first differences are not constant but the second differences are.

The nth term takes the form
$U_n = an^2 + bn + c$,
where b, c may be zero.

Finding the nth term of a quadratic sequence is a useful technique for when you are carrying out Investigational tasks for coursework

EXAMPLE
Find the nth term of 3, 9, 19, 33

term	1	2	3	4
number	3	9	19	33
1st difference		6	10	14
2nd difference			4	4

a is found by dividing the second difference by 2

nth term is $2n^2 + 1$

QUICK TEST

1. Write down the next two terms in the sequences below:

  a) 5, 7, 9, 11,___ , ___   b) 1, 4, 9, 16,___ , ___ c) 12, 10, 8, 6,___ , ___

2. Write down the nth term in the sequences below:

  a) 5, 7, 9, 11 . . .   b) 2, 5, 8, 11 . . .   c) 6, 10, 14, 18 . . .   d) 8, 6, 4, 2 . . .

1.a) 13, 15 b) 25, 36 c) 4, 2   2. a) 2n + 3 b) 3n – 1 c) 4n + 2 d) 10 – 2n

43

DRAWING STRAIGHT LINE GRAPHS

In order to draw a straight line graph follow these easy steps:-

STEP 1
Choose 3 values of χ and draw up a table.

STEP 2
Work out the value of y for each value of χ.

STEP 3
Plot the coordinates and join up the points with a straight line.

STEP 4
Label the graph.

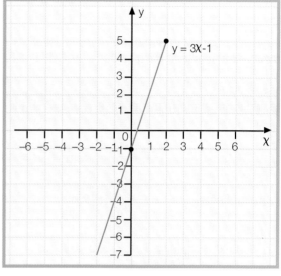

EXAMPLE
Draw the graph of y = 3χ − 1
1. Draw up a table with some suitable values of χ.

χ	−2	0	2
y	−7	−1	5

2. Work out the y values by putting each χ value into the equation.
e.g. χ = −2 ∴ y= 3 x −2 − 1
= −6 − 1
= −7

3. Plot the points and draw the line.

STRAIGHT LINE GRAPHS

FINDING THE GRADIENT OF A LINE

Do not count the squares as the scales may be different

- To find the gradient, choose two points.
- Draw a triangle as shown.
- Find the change in y (height) and the change in χ (base).
- gradient = $\frac{\text{change in y}}{\text{change in χ}}$ or $\frac{\text{height}}{\text{base}}$ = $\frac{4}{3}$ = $1\frac{1}{3}$
- Decide if the gradient is positive or negative.

GRAPHS OF Y = a, X = b

y = a is a horizontal line with every y coordinate equal to a.

X = b is a vertical line with every X coordinate equal to b.

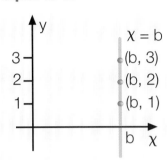

Examiner's Top Tip
You need to be able to sketch a straight line graph from its equation. If you can do this then you will be able to tell if the graph you have drawn is correct.

INTERPRETING y = mX + c

The general equation of a straight line graph is $y = mX + c$.

m is the gradient (steepness) of the line.

· As m increases the line gets steeper.
· If m is positive the line slopes forwards.
· If m is negative the line slopes backwards.

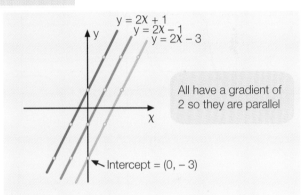

All have a gradient of 2 so they are parallel

Intercept = (0, − 3)

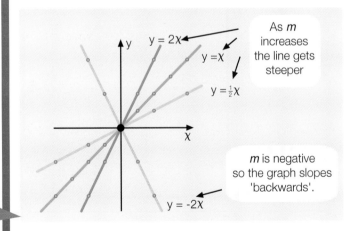

As *m* increases the line gets steeper

m is negative so the graph slopes 'backwards'.

c is the intercept on the y axis, that is, where the graph cuts the y axis.

Parallel lines have the same gradient.

If two lines are perpendicular the product of their gradient is −1.

If a line has a gradient of m, then a line which is perpendicular to it will have a gradient of $\frac{-1}{m}$

From the diagram the lines $y = -2X$ and $y = \frac{1}{2}X$ are perpendicular because $-2 \times \frac{1}{2} = -1$

QUICK TEST

1. Draw the graph of y = 6 – 2X. From your graph write down the solution of the equations:

   a) 6 – 2X = 4   b) 6 – 2X = 3

2. Write down the gradient and intercept for each of these straight line graphs:

   a) y = 4 + 2X   b) y = 3X – 2   c) 2y = 6X + 4

1. a) X = 1 b) X = 1.5   2. a) Gradient = 2, Intercept = (0, 4) b) Gradient = 3, Intercept = (0, −2) c) Gradient = 3, Intercept = (0,2)

CURVED GRAPHS

GRAPHS INVOLVING X^3 AND $\frac{1}{X}$

GRAPHS INVOLVING X^3

An equation of the form

$y = aX^3 + bX^2 + cX + d$

is called a <u>cubic</u> where a ≠ 0. For a > 0 the graph of a cubic takes one of these forms.

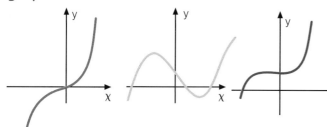

For a < 0 the overall trend is reversed.

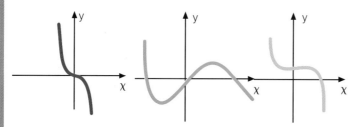

GRAPHS INVOLVING $\frac{1}{X}$

An equation of the form y = a/x takes two basic forms depending on the value of a.

a > 0

a < 0

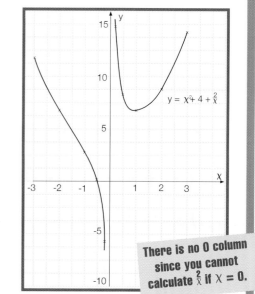

$y = X^2 + 4 + \frac{2}{X}$

There is no 0 column since you cannot calculate $\frac{2}{X}$ if X = 0.

EXAMPLE

Draw the graph of $y = X^2 + 4 + \frac{2}{X}$ for −3 ≤ X ≤ 3.

• Make a table of values:

X	−3	−2	−1	−0.5	−0.2	0.2	0.5	1	2	3
X^2	9	4	1	0.25	0.04	0.04	0.25	1	4	9
+4	4	4	4	4	4	4	4	4	4	4
$+\frac{2}{X}$	−0.$\dot{6}$	−1	−2	−4	−10	10	4	2	1	0.$\dot{6}$
y	12.$\dot{3}$	7	3	0.25	−5.96	14.04	8.25	7	9	13.$\dot{6}$

• Plot the points and draw a smooth curve. There will be a break in the curve at x = 0.

GRAPHS OF THE FORM $y = ax^2 + bx + c$

These are called <u>**quadratic**</u> <u>**graphs**</u> where $a \neq 0$.
These graphs are curved.
If $a > 0$ then the graph is shaped as shown.

If $a < 0$ then the graph is shaped as shown.

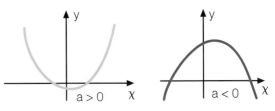

They are often known as parabolas.

EXAMPLE

Draw the graph of $y = x^2 - x - 6$ using values of x from –2 to 3.
Use the graph to find the value of x when $y = -3$.

• Make a table of values.

$x = 0.5$ is worked out to find the minimum value.

x	–2	–1	0	1	2	3	0.5
y	0	–4	–6	–6	–4	0	–6.25

• To work out the values of y substitute the values of x into the equation:
  e.g. If $x = 1$ $y = x^2 - x - 6$
                    $= 1^2 - 1 - 6$
                    $= -6$

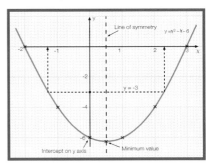

• Don't try and punch this all into your calculator at once. Do it step by step.
• Plot the points and join them with a <u>**smooth**</u> curve.

• The minimum value is when $x = 0.5$, $y = -6.25$.
• The line of symmetry is at $x = 0.5$.
• The curve cuts the y axis at (0, –6), i.e. (0, c).
• When $y = -3$, read across from $y = -3$ to the graph then read
  up to the x axis. $x = 2.3$ and $x = -1.3$. These are the approximate
  solutions of the equation $x^2 - x - 6 = -3$.

Show clearly on your graph how you take your readings.

- -

QUICK TEST

Examiner's Top Tip

Draw the curve with a sharp pencil, go through all the points and check for any parts that look wrong.

this point is obviously wrong

1. a) Complete the table of values for the graph $y = x^3 + 3$.

x	–3	–2	–1	0	1	2	3
y							

b) Draw the graph of $y = x^3 + 3$. Use scales of 1 unit per 2 cm on
   the x axis and 10 units per 2 cm on the y axis.

c) From the graph find the value of x when $y = 15$

2. Match each of the four graphs below with one of the following equations:

   a) $y = 2x - 5$ b) $y = x^2 + 3$ c) $y = 3 - x^2$ d) $y = 5 - x$ e) $y = x^3$ f) $y = \frac{2}{x}$

Graph A

Graph B

Graph C

Graph D

2. Graph A: $y = 3 - x^2$ Graph B: $y = \frac{2}{x}$ Graph C: $y = 5 - x$ Graph D: $y = x^3$
1. a)

x	–3	–2	–1	0	1	2	3
y	–24	–5	2	3	4	11	30

b) The coordinates that need to be plotted are: (3, 30), (2, 11), (1, 3), (0, 3), (–1, 2), (–2, –5), (–3, –24)
c) When $y = 15$, $x = 2.3$ (to 1.d.p)

HARDER WORK ON GRAPHS

SOLVING QUADRATIC AND LINEAR EQUATIONS SIMULTANEOUSLY

We have already seen that where two graphs meet, this represents the simultaneous solutions of the equations. So far we have only looked at linear equations, and their corresponding straight-lined graphs. You also need to be able to work out the coordinates of the points of intersection of a straight line and a quadratic curve.

The diagram shows the points of intersection of the straight line $y = 5x - 6$ and the curve $y = x^2$.

To find the coordinates of the points of intersection C and D of the line $y = 5x - 6$ and the curve $y = x^2$, we know that the points C and D both lie on the curve and the line.

$$y = 5x - 6 \qquad [1]$$
$$y = x^2 \qquad [2]$$

Eliminate y by substituting equation [2] into equation [1] (or by subtracting equation [1] from equation [2])

$$x^2 = 5x - 6$$
rearrange: $\qquad x^2 - 5x + 6 = 0$

factorise: $\qquad (x - 2)(x - 3) = 0$

so $\qquad x = 2$ and $x = 3$

(these are the x coordinates of the points of intersection)

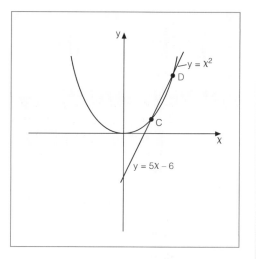

Substitute the values of x back in equation [1] to find the y coordinates.

$x = 2$ $\qquad y = 5x - 6$ $\quad$ Coordinate of C (2, 4)
$\therefore$ $\qquad\qquad y = 5 \times 2 - 6$
$\qquad\qquad\quad y = 4$

$x = 3$ $\qquad y = 5x - 6$ $\quad$ Coordinate of D (3, 9)
$\therefore$ $\qquad\qquad y = 5 \times 3 - 6$
$\qquad\qquad\quad y = 9$

So the line $y = 5x - 6$ intersects the curve $y = x^2$ at (2, 4) and (3, 9)

Examiner's Top Tip
Some quite difficult topics in this section. The four graph transformations need to be learnt – they often appear on the exam paper. Remember, solving a quadratic and a linear equation gives the point of intersection of the two graphs.

THE INTERSECTION OF A CIRCLE AND A LINE

The equation of a circle can be found by using Pythagoras' theorem.

The equation of any circle with centre (0, 0) and radius r is $x^2 + y^2 = r^2$.

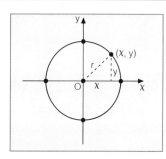

EXAMPLE

Find the coordinates of the points where the line $y - 5 = x$ cuts the circle $x^2 + y^2 = 25$.

The coordinates of the points of intersection must lie on the circle and the line. The coordinates must satisfy both equations:

$y - 5 = x$ $\quad$ [1] $\qquad x^2 + y^2 = 25$ $\quad$ [2]

rewrite equation [1] in the form 'y = '

$y = x + 5$ $\quad$ [1]

Eliminate y by substituting [1] into [2]

Expand brackets $x^2 + (x + 5)^2 = 25$

$\qquad\qquad x^2 + x^2 + 10x + 25 = 25$

rearrange $\quad 2x^2 + 10x = 0$

factorise $\quad 2x(x + 5) = 0$

so $\qquad x = 0$ or $x = -5$.

Substitute the values of x into equation [1] to find the values of y

$x = 0$ $\quad y = 0 + 5 = 5$

$x = -5$ $\quad y = -5 + 5 = 0$

The line $y = x + 5$ cuts the circle $x^2 + y^2 = 25$ at (0, 5) and (−5, 0)

Remember
$(x + 5)^2$ means
$(x + 5)(x + 5)$

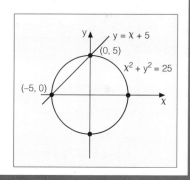

FUNCTIONS AND TRANSFORMATIONS

If y = an expression involving x then it can be written as $y = f(x)$
The graphs of related functions can be found by applying the following transformations.

1. $y = f(x) \pm a$ this is where the graphs move up or down the y axis by a value of a.

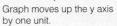
Graph moves up the y axis by one unit.

Graph moves down the y axis by one unit.

2. $y = f(x \pm a)$ **this is where the whole graph moves a units to the left or right. (They move in the opposite direction to what you would think!)**
$y = f(x + a)$ **moves the graph a units to the left.**
$y = f(x - a)$ **moves the graph a units to the right.**

Graph of $y = (x + 1)^2$ moves one unit to the left.

Graph of $y = (x - 1)^2$ moves to the right one unit.

3. $y = k \times f(x)$ **this is when the original graph stretches along the y axis by a factor of k.**
If $k > 1$ e.g. $y = 2x^2$ then all the points are stretched upwards in the y direction by a scale factor of 2
If $k < 1$ e.g. $y = \frac{1}{2}x^2$ then the graph squashes downwards by a scale factor of $\frac{1}{2}$.

For this graph the x values stay the same and the y values are multiplied by 2.

For this graph the x values stay the same and the y values are multiplied by $\frac{1}{2}$.

4. $y = f(kx)$ **this is sometimes confusing. If $k > 1$ then the graph stretches inwards in the x direction by $\frac{1}{k}$. For example if $y = (2x)^2$ then the x coordinates are multiplied by $\frac{1}{2}$. If $k < 1$ then the graph stretches outwards in the x direction by $\frac{1}{k}$. For example if $y = (\frac{1}{2}x)^2$ the x coordinates are multiplied by 2 ($1 \div \frac{1}{2} = 2$).**

For this graph the y coordinates stay the same and the x values are multiplied by $\frac{1}{2}$.

For this graph the y coordinates stay the same and the x values are multiplied by 2.

QUICK TEST

1 Sketch these graphs: a) $y = x^3$ b) $y = x^3 - 4$ c) $y = (x - 2)^3$ d) $y = 2x^3$

2 Solve the simultaneous equations $y = x^2$ and $y = 3x + 4$

2. $x = -1, y = 1$ $x = 4, y = 16$

1. (a) $y = x^3$ (b) $y = x^3 - 4$ (c) $y = (x-2)^3$ (d) $y = 2x^3$

DISTANCE–TIME GRAPHS

These are often called <u>travel graphs</u>.
The <u>speed</u> of an object can be found by finding the gradient of the line.
speed = <u>distance travelled</u>
             time taken

EXAMPLE

The graph shows Mr Rogers' car journey. Work out the speed of each stage.
a) The car is travelling at 30 m.p.h. for 1 hour (30 ÷ 1).
b) The car is stationary for 30 minutes.
c) The graph is steeper so the car is travelling faster, at a speed of 60 m.p.h. for 30 minutes (30 ÷ 0.5).
d) The car is stationary for 1 hour.
e) The return journey is at a speed of 40 m.p.h. (60 ÷ 1.5).

Examiner's Top Tip
Notice the importance of using the gradient of a line. It is useful to note that on the distance–time graph example, the scales on both axes are different. Care must be taken when reading the scales: always make sure you understand the scales before you start.

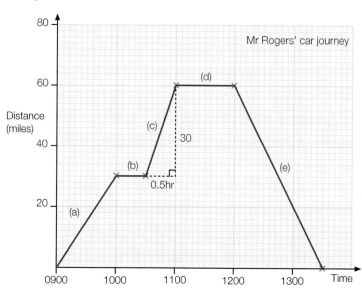

USING GRAPHS TO SOLVE EQUATIONS

A graph can be used to solve equations. Quite often the
equation needs to be rearranged in order to resemble the
equation of the plotted graph.

EXAMPLE

The graph $y = x^2 - 2x + 1$ is drawn opposite. Use your graph
to solve the following a) $x^2 - 2x + 1 = 6$ b) $x^2 - 3x = 0$

a) The equation needs to be arranged so that it is the
same as the plotted graph.
$x^2 - 2x + 1 = 6$
our graph is $x^2 - 2x + 1$ the solutions are simply where
$y = 6$ crosses the graph. $x = -1.35, 3.5$

b) We need to rearrange the equation:
$x^2 - 3x = 0$
$x^2 - 3x + x + 1 = x + 1$ (add $x + 1$ to both sides).
our graph is $y = x^2 - 2x + 1$

The solutions are where the graph crosses the line $y = x + 1$
$x = 0$ and $x = 3$

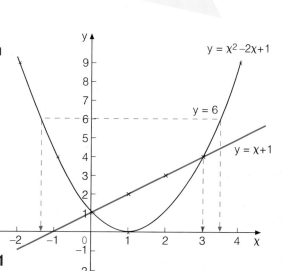

USING GRAPHS TO FIND RELATIONSHIPS

Sometimes you will be given a table of data which is known to fit a relationship. If a suitable graph is drawn the relationship can be found.

EXAMPLE

The graph below is known to fit the relationship $y = pq^x$. Use the graph to find the values of p and q and the relationship.

In order to find values for p and q we need to take values at R and S and then substitute them into the equation $y = pq^x$

At point R, $x = 0$ and $y = 4$

so $y = pq^x$ becomes
$4 = p \times q^0$ $(q^0 = 1)$
$4 = p$

At point S, $x = 2$ and $y = 16$

so $16 = 4 \times q^2$

$16 \div 4 = q^2$
$4 = q^2$
$q = \sqrt{4} = 2.$

The relationship is $y = 4 \times 2^x$

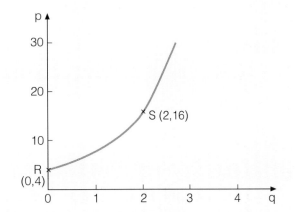

INTERPRETING GRAPHS

QUICK TEST

1.

A

B

C

1

2

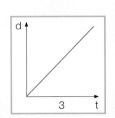
3

These containers are being filled with a liquid at a rate of 150 ml per second.

The graphs show how the depth of the water changes with time.

Match the containers with the graphs.

2. Draw the graph of $y = x^2 + x - 2$. Use your graph to solve the following:

a) $x^2 + x = 5$

b) $x^2 - 2 = 0$

c) $x^2 - 2x - 2 = 0$

EXAM QUESTIONS – Use the questions to test your progress. Check your answers on page 110.

1. Solve the following equations:
a) $2x + 4 = 10$ b) $3x - 1 = 11$ c) $5x - 3 = 2x + 12$ d) $3(x + 1) = 9$ e) $2(x + 1) = x + 3$

....

2. Here are the first five terms of a number sequence: 3, 9, 19, 33, 51.
Write down an expression for the nth term of the sequence.

....

3. Simplify:
a) $3x^2 \times 4x^2$ ....
b) $6x^2y \times 2x^3y^2$ ....
c) $12y^4 \div 3y$ ....
d) $(3y^2)^2$ ....

4. Solve the simultaneous equations:
$4a + 3b = 6$ ....
$2a - 3b = 12$ ....

(c) 5. $P^2 = 5xy - 3x^2$
a) Calculate the value of P when $x = 5.8$, $y = 105$ ....
b) Rearrange the formula $P^2 = 5xy - 3x^2$ to make y the subject ....

(c) 6. The equation $x^3 - 2x = 2$ has a solution between 1 and 2.
By using a method of trial and improvement, find this solution to 1 decimal place.

....

7. Solve the inequality $2 \leqslant 5n - 3 \leqslant 12$.

....

8. Match the graphs with the equations.
a) $y = x^2 - 4$ b) $y = 2x + 1$ c) $y = 3 - 4x$ d) $xy = 6$

A

B

C

D

....

9. Simplify:

a) $\dfrac{2}{(x + 4)} + \dfrac{3}{(x - 2)}$ b) $\dfrac{6}{x - 3} - \dfrac{2}{x + 4}$ c) $\dfrac{4a^2b}{a^4b} \times \dfrac{a^3b^2}{8ab^2}$

....

10. Factorise and then solve this quadratic equation $2x^2 - 13x + 18 = 0$

....

(c) Indicates that a calculator may be used

(c) 11. Solve by the quadratic formula

a) $3x^2 - 4x - 2 = 0$ b) $5x^2 - 3x - 1 = 0$

....

(c) 12. Solve by completing the square

a) $x^2 - 4x + 1 = 0$ ....

b) $x^2 - 8x + 10 = 0$ ....

13. If the area of the rectangle is 50 cm²

a) Show that $x^2 + x - 27 = 0$ ....

....

b) Work out the length of the rectangle.........................

....

(2x + 4) cm

| Area = 50 cm² | (x − 1) cm |

(c) 14. Solve the simultaneous equation and interpret your solution geometrically

$x^2 + y^2 = 16$ and $y = x + 4$.

15. Make p the subject of the formulae $6p + 2r = x(4-p)$ ....

16. Drawn below is the graph of $y = f(x)$

On separate axes draw the graphs of:

a) $y = f(x + 2)$
b) $y = f(x) - 3$
c) $y = -f(x)$
d) $y = f(2x)$

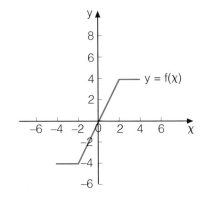

17. The graph is known to fit the relationship of $y = ab^x$.
Use the graph to find the value of a and b.

....

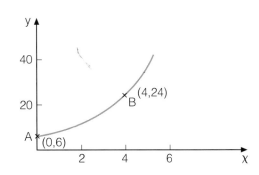

SYMMETRY

REFLECTIVE SYMMETRY

Both sides of a symmetrical shape are the same when the mirror line is drawn across it. The mirror line is known as the <u>line</u> or <u>axis of symmetry</u>.

1 line

1 line

3 lines

No lines

ROTATIONAL SYMMETRY

A 2D (two-dimensional) shape has rotational symmetry if, when turned, it looks exactly the same. <u>The order of rotational symmetry</u> is the number of times the shape turns and looks the same. For the letter M the shape has 1 position. It is said to have <u>rotational symmetry of order 1</u>, or no rotational symmetry.

Order 1

Order 1

Order 3

Order 4

PLANE SYMMETRY

This is symmetry in 3D (three-dimensional) solids only.
A 3D shape has a <u>plane of symmetry</u> if the plane divides the shape into two halves, and one half is an exact mirror image of the other.

Plane of symmetry

Examiner's Top Tip
When asked to draw in a plane of symmetry on a solid, make sure that it is a closed shape – don't just draw in a line of symmetry.

QUICK TEST

1. What are the names of the three types of symmetry?
2. The dashed lines are the lines of symmetry.
   Complete the shape so that it is symmetrical.
3. Draw a plane of symmetry on this solid.

3.

2.

3.

2. Plane, rotational, reflective
1. Plane, rotational, reflective

CONSTRUCTIONS

CONSTRUCTING A TRIANGLE

EXAMPLE

Use compasses to construct this triangle.
- Draw the longest side AB.
- With the compass point at A, draw an arc of radius 4 cm.
- With the compass point at B, draw an arc of radius 5 cm.
- Join A and B to the point where the two arcs meet at C.

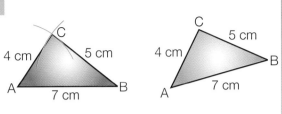

THE PERPENDICULAR BISECTOR OF A LINE

- Draw a line XY.
- Draw two arcs with the compasses, using X as the centre. The compasses must be set at a radius greater than half the distance of XY.
- Draw two more arcs with Y as the centre. (Keep the compasses the same distance apart as before.)
- Join the two points where the arcs cross.
- AB is the <u>perpendicular</u> <u>bisector</u> of XY.
- N is the <u>midpoint</u> of XY.

THE PERPENDICULAR FROM A POINT TO A LINE

From P draw arcs to cut the line at A and B.
From A and B draw arcs with the same radius to intersect at C.
Join P to C; this line is perpendicular to AB.

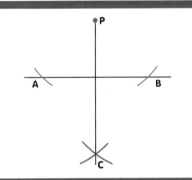

BISECTING AN ANGLE

- Draw two lines XY and YZ to meet at an angle.
- Using compasses, place the point at Y and draw the two arcs on XY and YZ.
- Place the compass point at the two arcs on XY and YZ and draw arcs to cross at N. Join Y and N. YN is the <u>bisector</u> of angle XYZ.

  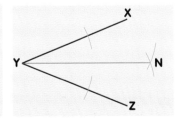

Examiner's Top Tip
Constructions are useful when answering locus questions and questions on scale drawings.

QUICK TEST

1. Bisect this angle.

2. Draw the perpendicular bisector of a 10 cm line.

2.

1.

ANGLE FACTS

Angles on a <u>straight</u> <u>line</u> add up to <u>180°</u>.
a + b + c = 180°

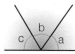

Angles at a <u>point</u> add up to <u>360°</u>.
a + b + c + d = 360°

Angles in a <u>triangle</u> add up to <u>180°</u>.
a + b + c = 180°

Angles in a <u>quadrilateral</u> add up to 360°.
a + b + c + d = 360°

<u>Vertically</u> <u>opposite</u> angles are <u>equal</u>.
a = b, c = d
a + d = b + c = 180°

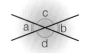

An <u>exterior</u> <u>angle</u> of a triangle equals the sum of the <u>two</u> opposite <u>interior</u> <u>angles</u>.
a + b = c

ANGLES ➡

READING ANGLES

When asked to find XYZ or ∠XYZ or XŶZ, find the <u>middle</u> <u>letter</u> angle, angle Y.

ANGLES IN PARALLEL LINES

<u>Alternate</u> **(z)** angles are <u>equal</u>.

<u>Corresponding</u> angles are <u>equal</u>.

<u>Supplementary</u> angles add up to 180°. c + d = 180°

EXAMPLES
Find the angles labelled by letters.

a = 50° + 70°
a = 120°

a + 80° + 40° + 85° = 360°
a = 360° – 205°
a = 155°

a = 120° (angles on a straight line)
b = 60° (vertically opposite)
c = 60° (corresponding to b or alternate to 60°)
d = 60° (vertically opposite to c)

POLYGONS

These are 2D shapes with <u>straight</u> sides.
<u>Regular</u> <u>polygons</u> are shapes with all sides and angles equal.

Number of sides	Name of polygon
3	Triangle
4	Quadrilateral
5	Pentagon
6	Hexagon
7	Heptagon
8	Octagon
9	Nonagon
10	Decagon

TESSELLATIONS

A <u>tessellation</u> is a pattern of 2D shapes which fit together without leaving any gaps.
For shapes to tessellate, the angles at each point must add up to 360°.

EXAMPLE
Regular pentagons will not tessellate.
Each interior angle is 108°, and
3 x 108° = 324°.
A gap of 360° – 324° = 36° is left.

108°
108° 108°
gap

 AN <u>ACUTE</u> ANGLE IS BETWEEN 0° AND 90°.

 AN <u>OBTUSE</u> ANGLE IS BETWEEN 90° AND 180°.

 A <u>REFLEX</u> ANGLE IS BETWEEN 180° AND 360°.

 A <u>RIGHT</u> ANGLE IS 90°.

ANGLES IN A POLYGON

There are two types of angle in a polygon: <u>interior</u> (inside) and <u>exterior</u> (outside).
For a regular polygon with n sides:
- sum of exterior angles = 360°, so exterior angle = $\frac{360°}{n}$
- interior angle + exterior angle = 180°
- sum of interior angles = (n – 2) x 180° or (2n – 4) x 90°.

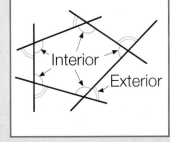
Interior
Exterior

EXAMPLE
A regular polygon has an interior angle of 150°.
How many sides does it have? Let n be the number of sides.
exterior + interior = 180°
exterior angle = 180° – 150° = 30°
But exterior angle = $\frac{360°}{n}$

So n = $\frac{360°}{\text{exterior angle}}$

n = $\frac{360°}{30°}$ = 12

Examiner's Top Tip
Make sure that you show full working out when carrying out an angle calculation. If you are asked to 'Explain', always refer to the angle properties, e.g. angles on a straight line add up to 180°, rather than how you worked it out.

QUICK TEST

1. Find the sizes of the angles below labelled by letters.

2. Find the size of an a) exterior and b) interior angle of a regular pentagon.

a.

b.

c.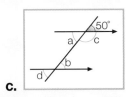

1. a) a = 150° b) b = 70°, c = 110°, d = 70°
c) a = 50°, b = 50°, c = 130°, d = 50°   2. a) 252° b) 108°

57

BEARINGS

- **A bearing is the direction travelled between two points, given as an angle in degrees.**
- **All bearings are measured clockwise from the north line.**
- **All bearings should be given as 3 figures, e.g. 225°, 043°, 006°.**

the bearing of A from B

EXAMPLES

Bearing of P from Q = 060°

Bearing of P from Q = 180° – 30° = 150°

Measure from the North Line at Q

Bearing of P from Q 360° – 50° = 310°

BACK BEARINGS

When finding the back bearing (the bearing of Q from P above):
- **draw in a north line at P;**
- **the two north lines are parallel lines, so the angle properties of parallel lines can be used.**

Bearing of Q from P = 60° + 180° = 240°

Bearing of Q from P = 360° – 30° = 330°

Measure from the north line at P

Bearing of Q from P = 180° – 50° = 130°

SCALE DRAWINGS AND BEARINGS

Examiner's Top Tip
The word _from_ is important when answering bearing questions. It tells you where to put the north line and where to measure.

Scale drawings are useful for finding lengths and angles.

EXAMPLE

A ship sails from a harbour for 15 km on a bearing of 040°, and then continues due east for 20 km. Make a scale drawing of this journey using a scale of 1 cm to 5 km. How far will the ship have to sail to get back to the harbour by the shortest route? What will the bearing be?

Shortest route = 6.4 x 5 km = 32 km
Bearing = 70° + 180° = 250°

Note – this diagram is not drawn accurately but is used to show you what your diagram should look like

SCALES AND MAPS

A scale of 1 : 25000 means that 1 cm on the scale drawing represents a real length of 25000 cm.

Scales are often used on maps. They are usually written as a ratio.

EXAMPLE

The scale on as road map is 1 : 25000. Bury and Oldham are 20 cm apart on the map.
Work out the real distance, in km, between Bury and Oldham.
Scale 1 : 25000, distance on map is 20 cm.
  Real distance = 20 x 25000 = 500000 cm
Divide by 100 to change cm to m.
  500000 / 100 = 5000 m
Divide by 1000 to change m to km.
  5000 / 1000 = 5 km

BEARINGS AND SCALE DRAWINGS

··

QUICK TEST

1. What are the bearings of A from B in the following:

a)

b)

c)

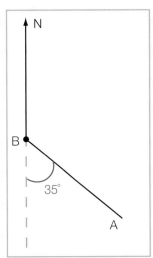

2. For each of the questions above work out the bearing of B from A.

3. The scale on a road map is 1 : 50000. If two towns are 14 cm apart on the map, work out the real distance between them.

1. a) 072° b) 305° c) 145°   2. a) 252° b) 125° c) 325°   3. 7 km

59

TRANSLATIONS

These move figures from one place to another. The size and shape of the figure are not changed. <u>Vectors</u> are used to describe the distance and direction of the translation.

A vector is written $\begin{bmatrix} a \\ b \end{bmatrix}$. a represents the <u>horizontal</u> movement, and <u>b</u> represents the <u>vertical</u> movement.

EXAMPLE

a) Translate ABC by the vector $\begin{bmatrix} 2 \\ 1 \end{bmatrix}$.
   Call it P.

b) Translate ABC by the vector $\begin{bmatrix} -3 \\ -2 \end{bmatrix}$.
   Call it Q.

This means 2 to the right and 1 upwards.

This means 3 to the left and 2 down.

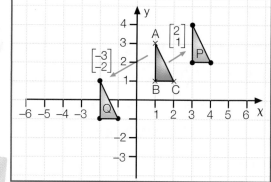

P and Q are <u>congruent</u>.

Remember that two shapes are <u>congruent</u> if one is exactly the same as the other.

TRANSFORMATIONS 1

REFLECTIONS

These create an image of an object on the other side of the mirror line. The mirror line is known as an <u>axis</u> <u>of</u> <u>reflection</u>. The size and shape of the figure are not changed.

EXAMPLE
Reflect triangle ABC in:
a) the χ axis, and call it D;
b) the line y = −χ, and call it E;
c) the line χ = 5, and call it F.
D, E and F are congruent to triangle ABC.

Count the squares of the object from the mirror; it's easier.

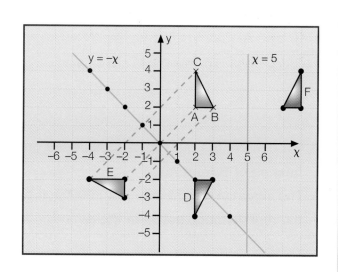

ROTATIONS

These **turn** a figure through an angle about some fixed point. This fixed point is called the **centre** **of** **rotation**. The size and shape of the figure are not changed.

EXAMPLE

Rotate triangle ABC:
a) 90° clockwise about (0, 0) and call it R;
b) 180° about (0, 0), and call it S;
c) 90° anticlockwise about (–1, 1), and call it T.

Examiner's Top Tip
When describing a rotation give:
• the centre of rotation
• the direction of the turn (clockwise/anticlockwise)
• the angle of the turn
Otherwise you will lose marks for not describing them fully.

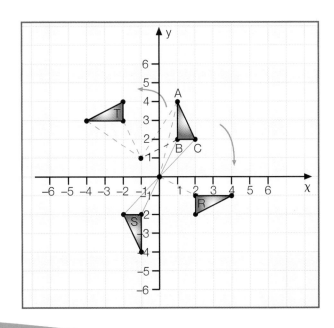

A **transformation** changes the **position** or **size** of a shape. There are four types of transformations: translations, reflections, rotations and enlargements.

QUICK TEST

1. On the diagram below:

a) Translate ABC by the vector $\begin{bmatrix} -3 \\ 1 \end{bmatrix}$
   Call it P

b) Reflect ABC in the line y = x. Call it Q

c) Reflect ABC in the line y = –1. Call it R

d) Rotate ABC 180° about (0, 0). Call it S

2. What does the vector $\begin{bmatrix} -2 \\ 3 \end{bmatrix}$ mean?

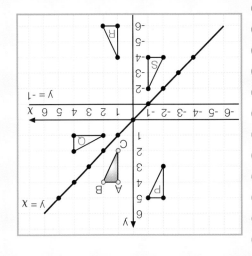

ENLARGEMENTS

These change the size but not the shape of an object.
The <u>centre of enlargement</u> is the point from which the enlargement takes place. The <u>scale factor</u> indicates how many times the lengths of the original figure have changed size.
• If the scale factor is <u>greater</u> <u>than</u> <u>1</u>, the shape becomes <u>bigger</u>.
• If the scale factor is <u>less</u> <u>than</u> <u>1</u>, the shape becomes <u>smaller</u>.

EXAMPLE
Enlarge triangle ABC by a scale factor of 2,
centre = (0, 0). Call it A'B'C'.

Notice each side of the enlargement is twice the size of the original.
A'B' = 2AB

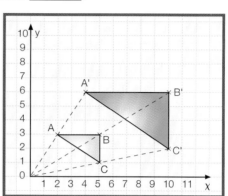

EXAMPLE
Describe fully the transformation that maps ABCDEF onto A'B'C'D'E'F'.
• To find the centre of enlargement, join A to A', and continue the line. Join B to B', and continue the line. Do the same for the others.
• Where all the lines meet is the centre of enlargement (–1, 3).
• The transformation is an enlargement with scale factor $\frac{1}{3}$. The centre of enlargement is at (–1, 3).

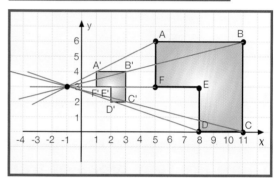

TRANSFORMATIONS ②

ENLARGEMENT WITH A NEGATIVE SCALE FACTOR

If the scale factor of an enlargement is negative, then the image is drawn on the opposite side of the centre of enlargement to the object. The image is also upside down.

EXAMPLE
Here ABC has been mapped onto
$A_1 B_1 C_1$ by a scale factor
of –2 centre at 0.

COMBINING TRANSFORMATIONS

These are a series of two or more transformations.

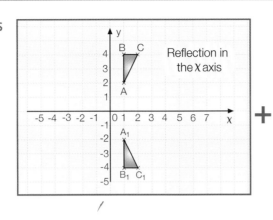
Reflection in the x axis

+

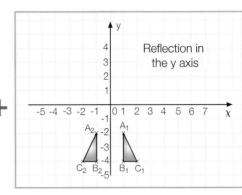
Reflection in the y axis

EXAMPLE

For triangle ABC:

a) Reflect ABC in the x axis. Call the image $A_1B_1C_1$.

b) Reflect $A_1B_1C_1$ in the y axis. Call the image $A_2B_2C_2$.

The single transformation that maps ABC onto $A_2B_2C_2$ directly is a rotation of 180°, centre (0, 0).

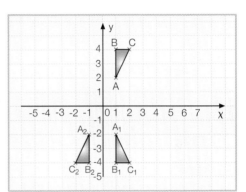

Examiner's Top Tip
When asked to describe an enlargement, you must include the scale factor and the position of the centre of enlargement.

- -

QUICK TEST

1. Draw an enlargement of shape P with a scale factor of 2, centre of enlargement as shown.

2. a) Rotate the shaded shape through a 90° clockwise rotation about (0, 0). Call this shape B.

   b) Reflect shape B in the x axis and call this shape C.

1.

Centre of enlargement

2.

P1

1.

SIMILARITY AND CONGRUENCY

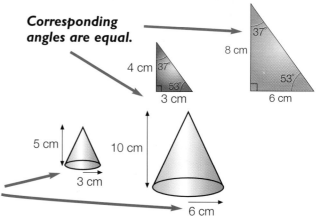

Similar figures are those which are the same shape but different sizes.
Corresponding angles are equal.
Corresponding lengths are in the same ratio.

EXAMPLES
Notice corresponding lengths are in the same ratio. The lengths of the bigger cone are twice the size of the smaller cone.

FINDING MISSING LENGTHS OF SIMILAR FIGURES

EXAMPLE
Find the missing length a, giving your answer to 2 s.f.

$\frac{9}{11} = \frac{9}{14}$ Corresponding sides are in the same ratio.

$a = \frac{9}{14} \times 11$ Multiply both sides by 11.

$a = 7.1$ cm (2 s.f.)

EXAMPLE
Calculate the missing length.

Measurements in cm

$\frac{X}{6} = \frac{24}{16}$ Corresponding sides are in the same ratio.

$X = \frac{24}{16} \times 6$ Multiply both sides by 6.

$X = 9$ cm

It is useful to draw the two triangles first.

Examiner's Top Tip
Always make sure you put the corresponding sides in the correct order and remember that whatever you are trying to work out must go on the top of the fraction otherwise you will have a tricky calculation to do.

CONGRUENT TRIANGLES

Two triangles are congruent if one of the following sets of conditions is true (S stands for side, A for angle, R for right angle, H for hypotenuse).

SSS – The three sides of one triangle are the same as the other.
SAS – Two sides and the angle between them in one triangle are equal to two sides and the included angle in the other.
RHS – Each triangle contains a right angle. The hypotenuse and another pair of sides are equal (RHS).
AAS – Two angles and a side in one triangle are equal to two angles and the corresponding side in the other.

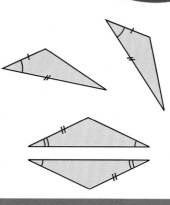

AREA AND VOLUMES OF SIMILAR FIGURES

Areas of similar figures are not in the same ratio as their lengths. For example, the corresponding lengths of these squares are in the ratio 1 : 2; their areas are in the ratio 1 : 4.

1

Hence if the corresponding lengths are in the ratio $a : b$ then their areas are in the ratio $a^2 : b^2$.

A similar result can be found when looking at the volume of similar objects. If the corresponding lengths are in the ratio $a : b$ then their volumes are in the ratio $a^3 : b^3$.

For a scale factor n

The sides are n times bigger.
The areas are n^2 times bigger.
The volumes are n^3 times bigger.

Examiner's Top Tip
When finding the area and volume of similar figures always try and work out the scale factor. Once you have calculated this the rest should be easy. If you are given the area or volume scale factor you may need to square or cube root them to find the linear scale factor.

EXAMPLE

These two shapes are similar. If the area of the smaller shape is 12 cm², calculate the area of the larger shape.

The linear scale factors are

$2.3 : 4.6$
$= 1 : 2$

Area scale factor is $\quad\quad 1^2 : 2^2$

Area of larger shape
$= 4 \times 12$
$= 48$ cm².

2.3 cm

4.6 cm

Area = 12 cm²

EXAMPLE

Two cones have surface areas of 9 cm² and 25 cm². Find the ratio of their volumes.

Area ratios are		$9 : 25$
so $a^2 : b^2$	=	$3^2 : 5^2$
i.e. $a : b$	=	$3 : 5$
Volume ratio $a^3 : b^3$	=	$3^3 : 5^3$
	=	$27 : 125$

QUICK TEST

1. Find the lengths labelled by the letters in these similar shapes

a)

b)

2. Two jugs are similar. One holds 100 cl and the other holds 200 cl. The 200 cl jug is 20 cm high. Calculate the height of the 100 cl jug.

3. Are these two triangles congruent? Explain why.

4. The heights of two similar shapes are 4 cm and 6 cm. If the area of the smaller shape is 40 cm², find the area of the larger shape.

4. Area = 90 cm².
3. Yes, congruent because SAS, i.e. 2 sides and included angle.
2. 15.9 cm
1. a) 7.8 cm b) 9.1 cm

LOCI AND COORDINATES IN 3D

The locus of a point is the set of all the possible positions which that point can occupy, subject to some given condition or rule.
The plural of locus is loci.

COMMON LOCI

- The locus of the points which are a constant distance from a fixed point is a circle. (i)
- The locus of the points which are equidistant from two points XY is the perpendicular bisector of XY. (ii)
- The locus of the points which are equidistant from two lines is the line which bisects the angle. (iii)
- The locus of the points which are a constant distance from a line XY is a pair of parallel lines above and below XY. (iv)

(i) Locus • P

(ii) Perpendicular bisector — X ⊥ Y

(iii) Locus

(iv) X——Y

> Draw the locus carefully and measure accurately.

EXAMPLE
A new hospital (H) is being built so that it is equidistant from the train station and the gas depot. The hospital cannot be within 80 m of the gas depot in case of a leak. Using a scale of 1 cm to 20 m, show the first available position for where the hospital can be built.

- Construct the perpendicular bisector between the train station and the gas depot.
- Draw a circle of radius 4 cm since nothing can be built within 80 m of the depot.
- The hospital (H) is shown.

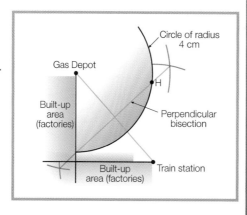

Circle of radius 4 cm

Gas Depot

Built-up area (factories)

Perpendicular bisection

Built-up area (factories)   Train station

> **Note – this is not drawn to scale but is used to show you what your diagram should look like.**

COORDINATES IN 3D

This involves the extension of the normal x – y coordinates into a third direction, known as z. All positions then have three coordinates (x, y, z).

EXAMPLE
For the cuboid the vertices would have the following coordinates:

A (3, 0, 0)
B (3, 2, 0)
C (0, 2, 0)
D (0, 2, 1)
E (0, 0, 1)
F (3, 0, 1)
G (3, 2, 1)
O (0, 0, 0)

3 cm, 1 cm, 2 cm

> **Examiner's Top Tip**
> When answering loci questions use the construction techniques previously shown: this will ensure your work is accurate.

QUICK TEST

1. A gold coin is buried in the rectangular field. It is:

a) 4 m from T

b) Equidistant from RU and RS

  Mark with an X the position of the gold coin

R —— 5 m —— S
2 m
U —————— T
Scale 1 cm : 1 m

4m, 45, 45

ANGLE PROPERTIES OF CIRCLES

CIRCLE THEOREMS

There are several theorems you need to know and be able to apply.
The theorems are:

1. The perpendicular bisector of any chord passes through the centre.

2. The angle in a semicircle is always 90°.

3. The radius and a tangent always meet at 90°.

4. Angles in the same segment are equal,
e.g. AB̂C = AD̂C

5. The angle at the centre is twice the angle at the circumference,
e.g. PÔQ = 2 x PR̂Q

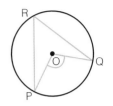

6. Opposite angles of a cyclic quadrilateral add up to 180°.
(A cyclic quadrilateral is a 4-sided shape with each corner touching the circle),
i.e.   X + y = 180°
         a + b = 180°

7. The lengths of two tangents from a point are equal,
e.g. RS = RT

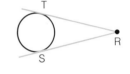

8. The angle between a tangent and a chord is equal to the angle in the alternate segment (that is the angle which is made at the edge of the circle by two lines drawn from the chord).
This is known as the Alternate Segment Theorem.
a = b.

Examiner's Top Tip
It is very important that you learn all of the eight theorems listed and that you can apply and explain them in the exam.

EXAM STYLE QUESTION

Calculate the angles marked with letters a – d in the diagram below

a = 140° (2 x angle at circumference)
b = ½(180° – 140°) (angles in an isosceles triangle)
   = 40° ÷ 2
   = 20°
c = 90° – 20°
(radius and tangent meet at 90°)
   = 70°
d = 180° – (2 x 70°)
(angles in an isosceles triangle PQR)
   = 40°

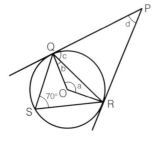

QUICK TEST

1. Calculate the missing angles in the diagram below.

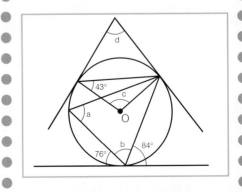

a = 84° b = 20° c = 94° d = 86°

FINDING THE LENGTH OF THE HYPOTENUSE

Remember: Pythagoras' theorem can only be used for right-angled triangles.

Step 1 Square the two numbers that you are given.

Step 2 To find the hypotenuse (longest side) **add** these two squared numbers.

Step 3 After adding the two lengths find the square root of your answer.

EXAMPLE
Find the length of AB, giving your answer to 1 decimal place.
Using Pythagoras' theorem gives:

$$AB^2 = AC^2 + BC^2$$
$$= 12^2 + 14.5^2$$
$$= 354.25$$
$$AB = \sqrt{354.25} \quad \text{Square root to find AB.}$$
$$= 18.8 \text{ m (to 1 d.p.)} \quad \text{Round to 1 d.p.}$$

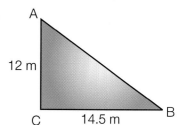

PYTHAGORAS' THEOREM

THE <u>HYPOTENUSE</u> IS THE LONGEST SIDE OF A RIGHT-ANGLED TRIANGLE. IT IS ALWAYS OPPOSITE THE RIGHT ANGLE.

SOLVING PROBLEMS

EXAMPLE
· Calculate the height of this isosceles triangle.

· Split the triangle down the middle to make it right-angled.
Using Pythagoras' theorem gives:
$$5^2 = h^2 + 1.75^2$$
$$h^2 = 5^2 - 1.75^2$$
$$h^2 = 21.9375$$
$$h^2 = \sqrt{21.9375} = 4.68 \text{ cm (to 2 d.p.)}$$

EXAMPLE
· A ladder of length 13 m rests against a wall.
The height up the wall the ladder reaches is 12 m.
How far away from the wall is the foot of the ladder?
$$13^2 = x^2 + 12^2$$
$$13^2 - 12^2 = x^2$$
$$169 - 144 = x^2$$
$$x^2 = 25$$
$$x = \sqrt{25} = 5 \text{ m}$$
The foot of the ladder is 5 m away from the wall.

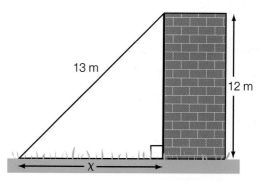

FINDING THE LENGTH OF A SHORTER SIDE

Follow the steps for finding the hypotenuse except:

Step 2 to find the shorter length subtract the smaller value from the larger value.

• Remember to square root ($\sqrt{}$) your answer.

EXAMPLE
Find the length of FG, giving your answer to 1 d.p.
Using Pythagoras' theorem gives:
$EF^2 = EG^2 + FG^2$
$FG^2 = EF^2 - EG^2$
$\quad = 27^2 - 18^2$
$\quad = 405$
$FG = \sqrt{405}$
$\quad = 20.1$ cm (to 1 d.p.)

Rearrange the formula:
use $a^2 = c^2 - b^2$

Examiner's Top Tip
Pythagoras' theorem allows us to calculate the length of one of the sides of a right-angled triangle, when the other two sides are known. If you are not told to what degree of accuracy to round your answer be guided by significant figures given in the question.

Pythagoras' theorem states: in any right-angled triangle, the square on the hypotenuse is equal to the sum of the squares on the other two sides.
Using the letters in the diagram, the theorem is written as:

$$c^2 = a^2 + b^2$$

This may be rearranged to give $a^2 = c^2 - b^2$ or $b^2 = c^2 - a^2$, which are useful when calculating one of the shorter sides.

CALCULATING THE LENGTH OF A LINE AB, GIVEN TWO SETS OF COORDINATES

By drawing in a triangle between the two points A (1, 2) and B (7, 6) we can find the length of AB by Pythagoras' Theorem.

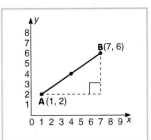

Horizontal distance = 6 (7 – 1)
Vertical distance = 4 (6 – 2)
Length of $(AB)^2 = 6^2 + 4^2$
$\quad\quad\quad (AB)^2 = 36 + 16$
$\quad\quad\quad (AB)^2 = 52$
$\quad\quad\quad\quad AB = \sqrt{52}$
Length of AB = 7.21

The midpoint of AB, M has coordinates (4, 4)
i.e. $\dfrac{(1 + 7)}{2}, \dfrac{2 + 6}{2}$

QUICK TEST

1. Calculate the lengths of the sides marked with a letter. Give your answers to 1 d.p.

a)

b)

2. Work out the length of the diagonal on this rectangle.

2.

3. A ship sets off from Port A and travels 50 km north then 80 km east to reach Port B. How far is Port A from Port B by the shortest route?

3.
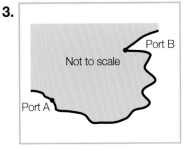

1. a) 17.2 cm b) 20.0 cm   2. 17 cm   3. 94.3 km

LABELLING THE SIDES OF THE TRIANGLE

hyp (hypotenuse) is opposite the right angle.
opp (opposite side) is opposite the angle θ.
adj (adjacent side) is next to the angle θ.

θ is a Greek letter called theta and is used to represent angles.

Opposite (opp)   Hypotenuse (hyp)
θ
(adj) Adjacent

TRIGONOMETRY IN RIGHT-ANGLED TRIANGLES

Trigonometry in right-angled triangles can be used to calculate an unknown angle or an unknown length.

TRIGONOMETRIC RATIOS

The three trigonometric ratios are:

$$\text{Sin } \theta = \frac{\text{opposite}}{\text{hypotenuse}}$$

$$\text{Cos } \theta = \frac{\text{adjacent}}{\text{hypotenuse}}$$

$$\text{Tan } \theta = \frac{\text{opposite}}{\text{adjacent}}$$

The made-up word

SOH CAH TOA

is a quick way of remembering the ratios. The word comes from the first letters of <u>S</u>in equals <u>O</u>pposite divided by <u>H</u>ypotenuse, etc.

To enter sin 30 into the calculator you usually do it backwards, i.e. **30** **SIN** (although some calculators do it forwards: check yours!)

CALCULATING THE SIZE OF AN ANGLE

EXAMPLE
Calculate angle AB̂C.
$\tan \theta = \frac{\text{opp}}{\text{adj}}$ Label the sides and decide on the ratio.

$\tan \theta = \frac{15}{27}$ Divide the top value by the bottom value.

$\tan \theta = 0.\dot{5}$

$\theta = 29.1° \text{ (1 d.p.)}$

To find the angle you usually use the second function on your calculator.

On the calculator type in

| 15 | ÷ | 27 | = | inv | tan | = |

You may have a shift key on your calculator.

A
hyp
opp 15 cm
θ
B
27 cm
adj
C

Examiner's Top Tip
Note – check your calculator as you may have to do it differently.

CALCULATING THE LENGTH OF A SIDE

EXAMPLE

Calculate the length of BC.
- Label the sides first.
- Decide on the ratio.
  $$\sin 30° = \frac{opp}{hyp}$$

- Substitute in the values.
  $$\sin 30° = \frac{BC}{25}$$

  $25 \times \sin 30° = BC$ Multiply both sides by 25.
  BC = 12.5 cm

Examiner's Top Tip
When calculating the size of an angle it should usually be rounded to 1 d.p. However do not round off your answer until right at the end of the question. You must learn the trigonometric ratios as they are no longer on the formula sheets.

EXAMPLE

Calculate the length of EF.
$$\cos 40° = \frac{adj}{hyp} = \frac{20}{EF}$$

$EF \times \cos 40° = 20$ Multiply both sides by EF.
$EF = \dfrac{20}{\cos 40°}$ Divide both sides by cos 40°.

  = 26.1 cm (1 d.p.)

20	÷	40	cos	=	or	20	÷	cos	40	=

QUICK TEST

1. Label the sides of these triangles with respect to θ.

a)

b)

c)

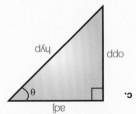
c.

2. Calculate the length of x in each triangle.

a)

b)

c)

b.

3. Work out the size of the angle in each of these triangles.

a)

b)

c)

a.

1. (see below)   2. a) 7.5 cm   b) 10.1 cm   c) 18 cm   3. a) 25.6°   b) 62.3°   c) 36.9°

SOLVING PROBLEMS INVOLVING THREE-DIMENSIONAL FIGURES

Problems involving three-dimensional figures very often have to be broken down into several stages. It is essential that the appropriate right angled triangles to be used are identified, the use of trigonometry and Pythagoras' theorem can then be applied.

EXAMPLE
The diagram shows a square based pyramid.
The point E lies directly above N.

a) Calculate the distance AC
b) Calculate the height of the vertex E above the base.
c) Calculate the angle between EC and the base ABCD.

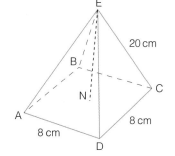

a) Triangle ADC contains a right angle at D.

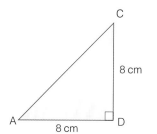

Using Pythagoras' theorem:
$AC^2 = AD^2 + DC^2$
$AC^2 = 8^2 + 8^2$
$AC^2 = 64 + 64$
$AC^2 = 128$
$AC = \sqrt{128}$
$AC = 11.31cm$ (to 2dp)

b) Triangle ENC contains a right angle at N.

Using Pythagoras' theorem:

$EC^2 = EN^2 + NC^2$

$EN^2 = EC^2 - NC^2$

$EN^2 = 20^2 - 5.65^2...$ (since $NC = \frac{1}{2}AC = \frac{11.31}{2}$

$EN^2 = 400 - 32$

$EN^2 = \sqrt{368}$

$EN = 19.18...cm$

c) Triangle ENC contains a right angle at N.

$\cos \theta = \dfrac{adj}{hyp}$

$\cos \theta = \dfrac{5.65....}{20}$

$\theta = \cos^{-1}\left(\dfrac{5.65...}{20}\right)$

$\theta = 73.6°$ (to 1dp)

The <u>angle of elevation</u> is measured from the horizontal <u>upwards</u>.

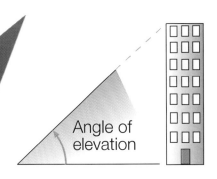

Angle of elevation

The <u>angle of depression</u> is measured from the horizontal <u>downwards</u>.

Angle of depression

APPLICATION OF TRIGONOMETRY

QUICK TEST

1. Dipak stands 30 m from the base of a tower. He measures the angle of elevation from ground level to the top of the tower as 50°. Calculate the height of the tower. Give your answer to 3 s.f.

1.

50°

30 m

tower

2. a) Calculate the length of BN.
   b) Calculate the length of BC.
   c) Calculate the size of ∠BCN.

2.

B

40 cm

30°

A   N   65 cm   C

3. The diagram shows a cuboid.
Calculate:
a) the length of HF
b) Angle CHF

3.

B   C

A   D

G

5 cm   F

15 cm

H   20 cm   E

b) Angle CHF =11.3°.
3. a) HF = 25cm
c) 17.1°
b) 68.0 cm
2. a) 20 cm
1. 35.8 m (3 s.f.)

FURTHER TRIGONOMETRY

THE SINE AND THE COSINE RULES

The sine and cosine rules allow you to solve problems in triangles which do not contain a right angle. Using these rules you should be able to calculate the length of an unknown side and the size of an unknown angle.

LABELLING THE TRIANGLE

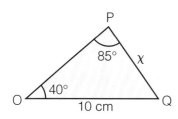

When labelling the triangle side a is opposite angle A side b is opposite angle B, etc.

THE SINE RULE

$$\frac{a}{\sin A} = \frac{b}{\sin B} = \frac{c}{\sin C}$$ or $$\frac{\sin A}{a} = \frac{\sin B}{b} = \frac{\sin C}{c}$$

when finding a length   when finding an angle

> ONLY TWO PARTS OF THE SINE RULE ARE USED AT ANY ONE TIME.

THE COSINE RULE

$$a^2 = b^2 + c^2 - 2bc \cos A$$ or $$\cos A = \frac{b^2 + c^2 - a^2}{2bc}$$

EXAMPLES

1. Calculate the length of PQ

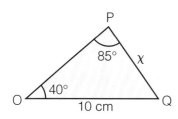

1) Call PQ, X, the length to be found.
2) Since we have <u>2 angles</u> and a <u>side</u>, we use the <u>Sine Rule</u>.
$$\frac{X}{\sin 40^\circ} = \frac{10}{\sin 85^\circ}$$
3) Rearrange to give: $X = \frac{10}{\sin 85} \times \sin 40^\circ$
Length of PQ = 6.5 cm (1dp).

2. Calculate the size of PQ̂O

1) Since we have <u>two sides</u> and an <u>angle NOT</u> enclosed by them we use the <u>Sine Rule</u>.
$$\frac{\sin Q}{15} = \frac{\sin 75^\circ}{20}$$
2) Rearrange to give $\sin Q = \frac{\sin 75^\circ}{20} \times 15$
$\sin Q = 0.7244\ldots$
$Q = \sin^{-1} 0.7244\ldots$
PQ̂O = 46.4° (1dp).

3. Calculate the length of FG

1) Call FG, X, the length to be found.
2) Since we have <u>two sides</u> and the <u>included angle</u> we use the <u>Cosine Rule</u>.
$X^2 = 9^2 + 10^2 - 2 \times 9 \times 10 \times \cos 65^\circ$.
$X^2 = 104.928\ldots$
$X = \sqrt{104.928\ldots}$
FG = 10.2 cm (1dp).

4. Calculate the size of angle FÊG

1) Since we have <u>all three sides</u> and no given angles we use the <u>Cosine Rule</u>.
$$\cos\theta = \frac{8^2 + 10^2 - 12^2}{2 \times 8 \times 10}$$
$\cos\theta = 0.125$
$\theta = \cos^{-1} 0.125$
FÊG = 82.8° (1dp).

Examiner's Tip
The Sine and Cosine Rule are key topics at GCSE. They usually are worth a great many marks and the key to success is to learn when you use the different rules. If in doubt and you have time try out the Sine and Cosine Rule on your triangle – you should find that one of them won't work.

GRAPHS OF TRIGONOMETRIC FUNCTIONS

The behaviour of the sine, cosine and tangent functions may be represented graphically as shown below.

1) y = sin X

The maximum and minimum values of sin X are 1 and −1. The pattern repeats every 360°.

2) y = cos X

The maximum and minimum values of cos X are 1 and −1. The pattern repeats every 360°. This graph is the same as y = sin X except it has been moved 90° to the left.

3) y = tan X

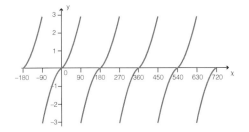

This graph is nothing like the two above. The values of tan X repeat every 180°. The tan of 90° is infinity, i.e. a value so great it cannot be written down.

Examiner's Tip
Practise drawing the trig graphs because you could be asked to sketch them in the exam.

OTHER EXAMPLES

1) y = a sin X

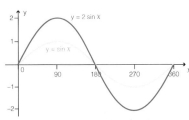

Here the points are stretched outwards in the y direction if a > 1. If a < 1 then they are pushed inwards.

2) y = sin bX

Here the points are pushed in the X direction if b < 1. If b > 1 then all the points are stretched outwards.

QUICK TEST

1. Calculate the missing length or angle marked X in the triangles below.

a)

b)

c)

d)

2. Find all the solutions of the equation sin X = $\frac{2}{3}$ in the range 0° ≤ X ≤ 360°.

The trigonometric graphs can be used to solve inverse problems.

EXAMPLE

For example to solve sin X = 0.5 for values of X between 0 and 360°, draw a straight line across at y = 0.5 and by its symmetrical properties we can see that the solutions are

X = 30°, 150°, (390° is out of the range)

METRIC UNITS

Length	Weight	Capacity
10 mm = 1 cm	1000 mg = 1 g	1000 ml = 1 l
100 cm = 1 m	1000 g = 1 kg	100 cl = 1 l
1000 m = 1 km	1000 kg = 1 tonne	1000 cm³ = 1 l

CONVERTING UNITS

- If changing from <u>small</u> units to <u>large</u> units (for example, g to kg), <u>divide</u>.
- If changing from <u>large</u> units to <u>small</u> units (for example, km to m), <u>multiply</u>.

EXAMPLES

(a) Change 50 mm into cm.
   mm are smaller than cm, so divide by the number of mm in a cm.
   50 ÷ 10 = 5 cm.
(b) Change 6 km into mm.
   km are bigger than mm, so multiply by the number of m in a km, cm in a m and mm in a cm.
   6 x 1000 x 100 x 10 = 6 000 000 mm.

km → m → cm → mm
x 1000   x 100   x 10

COMPOUND MEASURES

Speed can be measured in kilometres per hour (km/h), miles per hour (m.p.h.) and metres per second (m/s). km/h, m.p.h. and m/s are all <u>compound measures</u> because they involve a combination of basic measures.

SPEED

$$\text{average speed} = \frac{\text{total distance travelled}}{\text{total time taken}}$$

$$s = \frac{d}{t}$$

Always check the units first, before starting a question. Change them if necessary.

EXAMPLE

A car travels 50 miles in 1 hour 20 minutes. Find the speed in miles per hour.
Change the time units first:
20 minutes = $\frac{20}{60}$ of 1 hour
$$s = \frac{d}{t} = \frac{50}{1\frac{20}{60}} = 37.5 \text{ m.p.h.}$$

From the speed formula two other formulae can be found.
$$\text{time} = \frac{\text{distance}}{\text{speed}} \quad \text{distance} = \text{speed} \times \text{time}$$

$$s = \frac{d}{t} \qquad t = \frac{d}{s} \qquad d = st$$

Just remember the letters. It's quicker.

EXAMPLE

A car travels a distance of 240 miles at an average speed of 65 m.p.h. How long does it take?
$$\text{time} = \frac{\text{distance}}{\text{speed}} \text{ so } t = \frac{240}{65} = 3.692 \text{ hours}$$

3.692 hours must be changed to hours and minutes.
- Subtract the hours. So 3.692 – 3 = 0.692
- Multiply the decimal part by 60 minutes.
  0.692 x 60 = 42 minutes (nearest minute)
- Time = 3 hours 42 minutes.

DENSITY

$$\text{density} = \frac{\text{mass}}{\text{volume}} \qquad \text{volume} = \frac{\text{mass}}{\text{density}}$$

$$\text{mass} = \text{density} \times \text{volume}$$

$$D = \frac{M}{V} \qquad V = \frac{M}{D} \qquad M = DV$$

EXAMPLE

Find the density of an object whose mass is 400 g and whose volume is 25 cm³
$$\text{density} = \frac{M}{V} = = 16 \text{ g/cm}^3$$

Since the mass is in grams, volume is in cm³. Density is in g/cm³.

IMPERIAL UNITS

Length	Weight	Capacity
1 foot = 12 inches	**1 stone = 14 pounds (lb)**	**20 fluid oz = 1 pint**
1 yard = 3 feet	**1 pound = 16 ounces (oz)**	**8 pints = 1 gallon**

EXAMPLES

a) Change 4 yards into inches.
   Change yards to feet (x 3) and feet to inches (x 12).
   4 x 3 x 12 = 144 inches.
b) Change 166 pints into gallons.
   8 pints = 1 gallon, so 1 pint = $\frac{1}{8}$ gallon.
   166 ÷ 8 = 20.75 gallons.

COMPARISONS BETWEEN METRIC AND IMPERIAL UNITS

Length	Weight	Capacity
*2.5 cm ≈ 1 inch	*25 g ≈ 1 ounce	*1 litre ≈ $1\frac{3}{4}$ pints
*30 cm ≈ 1 foot	*1 kg ≈ 2.2 pounds	*4.5 litres ≈ 1 gallon
*1 m ≈ 39 inches		
*8 km ≈ 5 miles		

*All of the comparisons between metric and imperial units are only approximate.

EXAMPLE

Change 25 km into miles.
8 km ≈ 5 miles.
1 km ≈ $\frac{5}{8}$ mile = 0.625 miles.
25 km ≈ 25 x 0.625
= 15.625 miles.

Examiner's Top Tip
There is a lot of learning to do in this section. Try and learn all the
- metric and imperial conversions,
- formulas for speed, distance and time. Use the formula triangle to help you.

D
S x T

MEASURES AND MEASUREMENT

ACCURACY OF MEASUREMENT

There are two types of measurements: discrete measurements and continous measurements.

DISCRETE MEASURES
These are quantities that can be counted; for example, the number of baked bean tins on a shelf.

CONTINUOUS MEASURES
These are measurements which have been made by using a measuring instrument; for example, the height of a person. Continuous measures are <u>not exact</u>.

EXAMPLE
Nigel weighs 72 kg to the nearest kg. His actual weight could be anywhere between 71.5 kg and 72.5 kg.

71 kg   71.5 kg   72 kg   72.5 kg   73 kg

−0.5   +0.5

These two values are the <u>limits</u> of Nigel's weight.

If W represents weight, then

$$71.5 \leq W < 72.5$$

This is the <u>lower limit</u> of Nigel's weight (sometimes known as the <u>lower bound</u>). Anything below 71.5 would be recorded as 71 kg.

This is the <u>upper</u> <u>limit</u> (<u>upper bound</u>) of Nigel's weight. Anything from 72.5 upwards would be recorded as 73 kg.

> In general, if a measurement is accurate to some given amount, then the true value lies within a maximum of a half a unit of that amount.

EXAMPLE
The length of a seedling is measured as 3.7 cm to the nearest tenth of a cm. What are the upper and lower limits of the length?

3.6   3.65   3.7   3.75   3.8

−0.05   +0.05

lower limit $3.65 \leq L < 3.75$ upper limit

QUICK TEST

1. Change 3500 g into kg.
2. Change 3 kg into pounds.
3. Change 6 litres into pints.
4. Write down the upper and lower limits for a time of 9.2 seconds, rounded to the nearest tenth of a second.
5. Write down the upper and lower limits for a weight of 58 kg, rounded to the nearest kg.
6. Amy walks 6 miles in 2 hours 40 minutes. Find her average speed.
7. Find the time taken for a car to travel 600 miles at an average speed of 70 m.p.h.
8. Find the density of an object whose mass is 20 g and whose volume is 9 cm³.

8. 2.2 g/cm³
1. 3.5 kg 2. 6.6 lb 3. 10½ pints 4. $9.15 \leq 9.2 < 9.25$ 5. $57.5 \leq 58 < 58.5$ 6. 2.25 m.p.h. 7. 8.57 hours (or 8 hours 34 minutes)

AREAS OF QUADRILATERALS AND TRIANGLES

AREA OF A RECTANGLE
Area = length x width
$A = l \times w$

AREA OF A PARALLELOGRAM
Area = base x perpendicular height
Remember to use the perpendicular height, not the slant height.
$A = b \times h$

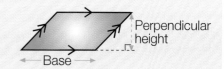

AREA OF A TRIANGLE
Area = $\frac{1}{2}$ base x perpendicular height
$A = \frac{1}{2} \times b \times h$

AREA OF A TRAPEZIUM
Area = $\frac{1}{2}$ x (sum of parallel sides) x perpendicular height between them
$A = \frac{1}{2} \times (a + b) \times h$

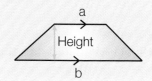

EXAMPLES
Find the areas of the following shapes, giving the answers to 3 s.f. where necessary. (Note: the 5 cm length is NOT used.)

a) $A = b \times h$
  $= 12 \times 4$
  $= 48$ cm²

b) $A = \frac{1}{2} \times (a + b) \times h$
  $= \frac{1}{2} \times (4.9 + 10.1) \times 6.2$
  $= 46.5$ cm²

EXAMPLE
If the area of this triangle is 55 cm², find the height, giving your answer to 3 s.f.

$A = \frac{1}{2} \times b \times h$
$55 = 1/2 \times 16.9 \times h$
$55 = 8.45 \times h$
$\frac{55}{8.45} = h$

Substitute the values into the formula.
Divide both sides by 8.45.
So h = 6.51 cm (to 3 s.f.)

Examiner's Top Tip
You have got lots more formulae to learn here. You need to know all these formulae (except the trapezium), otherwise you will find answering the questions very difficult.

CHANGING AREA UNITS

EXAMPLE
The square has a length of 1 metre.

This is the same as a length of 100 cm.
Area = 1 m²   Area = 10 000 cm²
Therefore 1 m² = 10 000 cm² (not 100 as most people think!)
Because of this possible mistake it's always better to change the units before you start a question.

CIRCUMFERENCE AND AREA OF A CIRCLE

circumference	= π x diameter C = π x d
	= 2 x π x radius = 2 x π x r
area	= π x (radius)² A = π x r²

EXAMPLE

The diameter of a circular rose garden is 5 m.
Find the circumference and area of the rose garden.

C = π x d   Substitute in the formula.
= 3.14 x 5   Use π = 3.14 or
                   the value of π on
                   your calculator.
= 15.7 m   EXP often gives the
                   value of π.

5 m

When finding the area, work out the radius first.
d = 2 x r so r = d ÷ 2, and r = 2.5 m
A = π x r²
= 3.14 x 2.5²   Remember 2.5² means 2.5 x 2.5.
= 19.625
= 19.6 m² (3 s.f.)

Note – this answer could be left as 6.25π, i.e. in terms of π

EXAMPLE

A circle has an area of 40 cm². Find the radius of
the circle, giving your answer to 3 s.f. Use π = 3.14.

A = π x r²
40 = 3.14 x r²   Substitute the values into
                        the formula.
$\frac{40}{3.14}$ = r²   Divide both sides by 3.14.

r² = 12.738 . . .
r = √12.738 . . .Take the square root to find r.
= 3.57 cm (3 s.f.)

Remember r² means r x r

AREA OF 2D SHAPES

PERIMETER AND AREA OF 2D SHAPES

Perimeter: this is the distance around the outside edge of a shape.

Area: this is the amount of space a 2D shape covers.

Common units of area are mm², cm², m², etc.

QUICK TEST

Work out the areas of the following shapes, giving your answers to 3 s.f.

1. a)

4.2 cm
8.1 cm
12.6 cm

b)

5.3 cm
12 cm

c)

9 cm

d)

8 cm
15 cm

2. Work out the area
   of the shaded region.

10 cm

2. 21.5 cm² (3 s.f.)

1. a) 68.0 cm² (3 s.f.) b) 63.6 cm² (3 s.f.) c) 63.6 cm² (3 s.f.) d) 208 cm² (3 s.f.)

VOLUME OF PRISMS

> A prism is any solid which can be cut into slices, which are all the same shape. This is called having a uniform cross-section.

VOLUME OF A CUBOID

volume =
length x width x height
$V = l \times w \times h$

Height
Width
Length

VOLUME OF A PRISM

volume = area of
cross-section x length
$V = a \times l$

Length
Area of cross section

VOLUME OF A CYLINDER

Cylinders are prisms where the cross-section is a circle.
volume = area of cross-section x length

$V = \pi r^2 \times h$

Radius
Height
area of circle
height or length

> To find the surface area of a cuboid work out the area of each face and then add them together

EXAMPLES

Find the volumes of the following 3D shapes, giving the answer to 3 s.f. Use $\pi = 3.14$.

> The area of cross-section is the area of a triangle.

7 cm
9.6 cm
15.1 cm

a) $V = a \times l$
$= (\frac{1}{2} \times b \times h) \times l$
$= (\frac{1}{2} \times 9.6 \times 7) \times 15.1$
$= 507.36 \text{ cm}^3$
$= 507 \text{ cm}^3$ (3 s.f.)

b) $V = \pi r^2 \times h$
$= 3.14 \times 10.7^2 \times 24.1$
$= 8663.92 \text{ cm}^3$
$= 8660 \text{ cm}^3$ (3 s.f.)

10.7 cm
24.1 cm

EXAMPLE

If the volume of the cylinder is 500 cm³, work out the radius. (Use $\pi = 3.14$.)

9.7 cm
r

$V = \pi r^2 \times h$
$500 = 3.14 \times r^2 \times 9.7$ — Substitute into the formula.

$500 = 30.458 \times r^2$

$\dfrac{500}{30.458} = r^2$ — Divide both sides by 30.458.

$r^2 = 16.416 \ldots$ — Take the square root to find the radius.

$r \quad \sqrt{16.416 \ldots}$ — So r = 4.05 cm (3 s.f.)

GCSE SAMPLE QUESTION

Here are some expressions.

$4\pi r^2$	$\frac{4}{5}pq^2$	$\sqrt{p^2 + q^2}$	$\pi p^2 q$	$\frac{5}{6}(pqr)$
✓	Volume	Length	Volume	Volume

$q(\sqrt{p^2 + r^2})$	$\pi/5\,(q^2 r)$	$\dfrac{\pi p^2 r}{q}$	$\dfrac{4\pi r^3}{pq}$
✓	Volume	✓	Length

The letters p, q and r represent length. π, 4, 5 and 6 are numbers that have no dimensions. Three of the expressions represent area. Tick the boxes underneath (✓) these three expressions.

> $\sqrt{p^2 + q^2}$ is a formula for perimeter or length.

> $q(\sqrt{p^2 + r^2})$ is length x length hence this is formula for area.

> All formulae for area have the dimensions length x length. For example, $4\pi r^2$ can be written as
> $4 \times \pi \times r \times r$
> (no dimensions x length x length)
> therefore it is a formula for area.

CONVERTING VOLUME UNITS

Another tricky topic which usually catches everybody out!

EXAMPLE

The cube has a length of 1 m – this is the same as a length of 100 cm.
Therefore $1 \text{ m}^3 = 1\,000\,000 \text{ cm}^3$

Not quite what you may think!

It's probably better therefore to change all the lengths to the same unit before starting a question!

1 m
1 m
1 m
volume = 1 m³

100 cm
100 cm
100 cm
volume = 1 000 000 cm³

VOLUME OF 3D SHAPES

VOLUME: THIS IS THE AMOUNT OF SPACE A 3D SHAPE OCCUPIES. COMMON UNITS OF VOLUME ARE MM³, CM³, M³, ETC.

Examiner's Top Tip
For any volume question work out carefully, check that you show full working out and show each step in your working.

DIMENSIONS

- The dimension of <u>perimeter</u> is <u>length</u> (L); it is a measurement in one dimension.
- The dimension of <u>area</u> is <u>length</u> x <u>length</u> ($L \times L = L^2$); it is a measurement in two dimensions.
- The dimension of <u>volume</u> is <u>length</u> x <u>length</u> x <u>length</u> ($L \times L \times L = L^3$); it is a measurement in three dimensions.
- Values like 3, $\frac{4}{\pi}$, 6.2, etc. have no dimensions.

EXAMPLES

The letters a, b, c and d all represent lengths. For each expression, write down whether it represents a length, area or volume.

a) $a^2 + b^2$ = (length x length) + (length x length) = area
$$\underline{L^2} + \underline{L^2}$$

b) $\frac{1}{3} \pi abc$ = number x length x length x length = volume
$$\underline{L^3}$$

c) $2\pi a + \frac{3}{4}\pi d$ = (number x length) + (number x length) = length
$$\underline{L} + \underline{L}$$

d) $\frac{5}{9}\pi a^2 d + \pi b^2 c^2$ = (number x length x length x length) + (number x length² x length²) = none
$$\underline{L}^3 + \underline{L}^4$$

A formula with a mixed dimension is impossible.

A dimension greater than 3 is impossible, so it has no dimension.

QUICK TEST

1. Work out the volumes of the following 3D shapes. Give your answer to 3 s.f.

a) 6.5 cm, 19.8 cm, 27.2 cm

b) 85 cm, 10.6 cm

2. The volumes of a cylinder is 2000 cm³ and the radius is 5.6 cm. Work out the height to 3 s.f.

3. x, y, z represent lengths. For each expression write down whether it could represent perimeter, area or volume.

a) $\sqrt{x^2} + \sqrt{y^2} + \sqrt{z^2}$

b) $\frac{5}{9}\pi x^3 + 2y^3$

c) $\frac{1}{3}\frac{xyz^2}{y}$

d) $\frac{9}{5}\pi xy + \frac{4}{5}\pi yz$

1. a) 1750 cm³ (3 s.f.) b) 60100 cm³ (3 s.f.)   2. 20.3 cm (3 s.f.)   3. a) Perimeter b) Volume c) Volume d) Area

FURTHER LENGTH, AREA AND VOLUME

On the higher tier paper you are required to find the area and volume of more complex shapes and solids. Some of the formulae you will be given but the others you will need to learn.

ARC LENGTH, SECTOR AREA AND AREA OF A SEGMENT

LENGTH OF A CIRCULAR ARC
This can be expressed as a fraction of the circumference of the circle.

Length of arc $= \dfrac{\theta}{360°} \times \pi \times r \times 2$ — This is the circumference of the circle.

$= \dfrac{70°}{360°} \times \pi \times 10 \times 2$

$= 12.22$ cm (1dp)

AREA OF A SECTOR
This can be expressed as a fraction of the area of the circle.

Area of a sector $= \dfrac{\theta}{360°} \times \pi r^2$ — This is the area of the circle.

$= \dfrac{70°}{360°} \times \pi \times 10^2$

$= 61.1$ cm² (1dp)

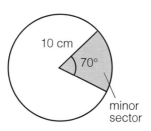

AREA OF A TRIANGLE
If we know the length of two sides of a triangle and the included angle we can find the area.

Area $= \frac{1}{2} \times c \times b \times \sin A$ — included angle

two lengths

Area $= \frac{1}{2} \times 6.9 \times 10.4 \times \sin 30°$

Area $= 17.9$ cm² (1dp)

AREA OF A SEGMENT
This can be worked out in two stages.
1. Calculate the area of the sector and the area of the triangle.
2. Subtract the area of the triangle from the area of the sector.

Segment area $= \left(\dfrac{70°}{360°} \times \pi \times 10^2\right) - \left(\frac{1}{2} \times 10 \times 10 \times \sin 70°\right)$

$= 61.09 - 46.98$

$= 14.1$ cm² (1dp)

Examiner's Top Tip
On the non-calculator paper you could easily be asked to find the volume of a solid. Don't be put off when it says leave your answer in terms of π, that just means leave the π in your calculation instead of working it out. Always show full working out and learn the formulae.

SPHERES, PYRAMIDS AND CONES

SPHERE

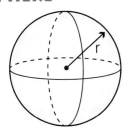

Volume of a sphere	$= \frac{4}{3}\pi r^3$
Surface area of a sphere	$= 4\pi r^2$

EXAMPLE

Find the volume and surface area of a sphere of radius = 10 cm.

$V = \frac{4}{3} \times \pi \times r^3$

$V = \frac{4}{3} \times \pi \times 10^3$

$= \frac{4000}{3} \times \pi \ cm^3$

$= 4190 \ cm^3$ (3sf)

On the non-calculator exam you may be asked to leave your answer in terms of π

Surface area $= 4 \times \pi \times r^2$

$= 4 \times \pi \times 10^2$

$= 400 \ \pi \ cm^2$

$= 1260 \ cm^2$ (3sf)

PYRAMIDS AND CONES

A cone is simply a pyramid with a circular base.

Volume of a pyramid	$= \frac{1}{3} \times$ area of base $\times$ height
Volume of a cone	$= \frac{1}{3} \times \pi \times r^2 \times$ height
Curved surface area of a cone	$= \pi r l$

(l is the slant height)

EXAMPLE

Calculate:

(i) the volume
(ii) the total surface area of the cone.

(i) volume $= \frac{1}{3} \times \pi \times 6^2 \times 8 = 96\pi \ cm^3 = 301.6 \ cm^3$

(ii) total surface area $=$ curved surface area $+$ area of circle

$l = \sqrt{8^2 + 6^2}$ $\pi \times 6 \times 10$ $+$ $\pi \times 6^2$

$l = \sqrt{100}$ 60π $+$ 36π

$l = 10 \ cm$ total area $= 96\pi = 301.6 \ cm^2$

QUICK TEST

1. Calculate the arc length and sector area of AOB.

2. Calculate the total volume of this solid, leaving your answer in terms of π.

1. Arc length = 13.96 cm. Sector area = 139.6 cm²   2. 123 π cm³.

83

IMPORTANT POINTS

Vectors **have both distance and direction. Four types of notation are used to represent vectors.**

The vector shown here can be referred to as:

$\begin{pmatrix} 3 \\ 2 \end{pmatrix}$ **or** *a* **or** $\underline{a}$ **or** $\vec{AB}$

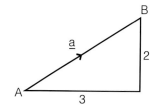

The direction of the vector is shown on the diagram by using an arrow.

If two vectors are equal then they are parallel and equal in length.

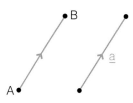

If $\vec{AB} = k\vec{DE}$ **then** $\vec{AB}$ **and** $\vec{DE}$ **are parallel and the length of** $\vec{AB}$ **is** *k* **times the length of** $\vec{DE}$**.**

$\vec{CD} = 2\vec{AB}$

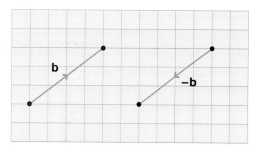

If the vector $b = \begin{pmatrix} 4 \\ 3 \end{pmatrix}$ **then**
The vector –*b* **is in the opposite direction to** *b*

$-b = -1 \times b = \begin{pmatrix} -4 \\ -3 \end{pmatrix}$

The *magnitude* **of a vector is the length of the directed line segment representing it. If the vector is expressed in column form, then Pythagoras' theorem can be used to find the magnitude.**

In general the magnitude of a vector $\begin{pmatrix} x \\ y \end{pmatrix}$ **is** $\sqrt{x^2 + y^2}$

The magnitude of AB is given by:

$$AB^2 = 3^2 + 4^2$$
$$AB^2 = 9 + 16$$
$$AB^2 = 25$$
$$AB = \sqrt{25}$$
$$AB = 5$$

The magnitude of $\vec{AB}$ **is 5 units.**

ADDING AND SUBTRACTING VECTORS

The *resultant* **of two vectors is found by adding them. Vectors must always be added end to end so that the arrows follow on from each other. A resultant is usually labelled with a double arrow.**

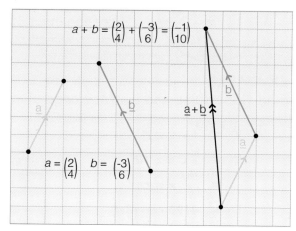

$$a + b = \begin{pmatrix} 2 \\ 4 \end{pmatrix} + \begin{pmatrix} -3 \\ 6 \end{pmatrix} = \begin{pmatrix} -1 \\ 10 \end{pmatrix}$$

$$a = \begin{pmatrix} 2 \\ 4 \end{pmatrix} \quad b = \begin{pmatrix} -3 \\ 6 \end{pmatrix}$$

Vectors can also be subtracted.
a **-** *b* **can be interpreted as** *a* **+** *(-b)*

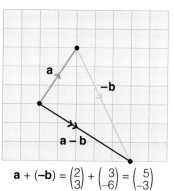

$$a + (-b) = \begin{pmatrix} 2 \\ 3 \end{pmatrix} + \begin{pmatrix} 3 \\ -6 \end{pmatrix} = \begin{pmatrix} 5 \\ -3 \end{pmatrix}$$

SPLITTING VECTORS INTO COMPONENTS

Any vector can be split into two components that are at 90° to each other. These two components will be *F cos θ* **and** *F sin θ*.

POSITION VECTORS

The position vector of a point P is the vector $\vec{OP}$ **where O is the origin.**

In the diagram the position vectors of C and D are *c* **and** *d* **respectively.**

Using this notation:

1) $\vec{CD} = -c + d$ **or** *d* – *c*

2) $\vec{OM} = c + \frac{1}{2}(d - c)$
$\qquad = \dfrac{d + c}{2}$
where M is the midpoint of CD

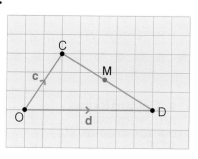

TYPICAL GCSE QUESTIONS

EXAMPLE 1

Given that $\vec{OA}$ = a
$\vec{OB}$ = b, $\vec{OC}$ = c
and that N splits $\vec{AB}$
in the ratio 1:2, find
the following vectors:

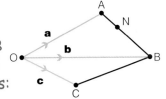

i) $\vec{AC}$ = -a + c (go from A to C via O)

ii) $\vec{AB}$ = -a + b (go from A to B via O)

iii) $\vec{CB}$ = -c + b (go from C to B via O)

iv) $\vec{AN}$ = $\frac{1}{3}\vec{AB}$ = $\frac{1}{3}$(-a + b)

v) $\vec{ON}$ = a + $\frac{1}{3}$(-a + b) = $\frac{2}{3}$a + $\frac{1}{3}$b = $\frac{1}{3}$(2a + b)

(go via A)

EXAMPLE 2

Thomas canoes across a river. In still
water, the canoe travels at 6 m/s.
The current of the river is 3 m/s.

Just add the two velocity
vectors end to end.

Calculate
a) The resultant speed of the canoe.
b) The angle between the direction of
the canoe and the current.

a) Resultant speed =
$$AB^2 = 6^2 + 3^2$$
$$= 36 + 9$$
$$AB = \sqrt{45}$$
$$= 6.71 \text{ m/s (2dp)}$$

b) Direction
$$\tan \theta = \frac{6}{3}$$
$$\theta = \tan^{-1}(2)$$
$$= 63.43° \text{ (2dp)}$$

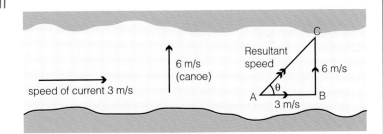

Examiner's Top Tip

Care needs to be taken when
answering vector questions. Always
check that the vectors you are using
are end to end so that all the arrows
point with each other (i.e. in the
same direction) and not opposite
each other. Always try and
simplify your answer as in
Example1 part (v).

Vectors

QUICK TEST

1. $\vec{AB}$ = $\binom{2}{3}$, $\vec{BC}$ = $\binom{4}{5}$, $\vec{PQ}$ = $\binom{3}{4}$

a) Show that $\vec{AC}$ is parallel to $\vec{PQ}$.

b) Write down the ratio of the length of AC to the length of PQ.

2. PQR is an equilateral triangle.

   M is the midpoint of PR.

$\vec{PQ}$ = p

$\vec{QR}$ = q

Work out in terms of p and q expressions for the vectors:

a) $\vec{PR}$ b) $\vec{MQ}$

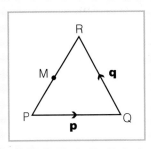

2. a) $\vec{PR}$ = p + q   b) $\vec{MQ}$ = $\frac{1}{2}$(p − q)
b) Ratio 2:1
1. a) Since $\vec{AC}$ = $\binom{6}{8}$ and $\vec{PQ}$ = $\binom{3}{4}$ then 2 $\vec{PQ}$ = $\vec{AC}$ so they are parallel.

EXAM QUESTIONS – Use the questions to test your progress. Check your answers on page 110–111.

1. Draw the image of the shaded shape after an enlargement by the scale factor $\frac{1}{2}$, with C as the centre of enlargement.
Label the image R.

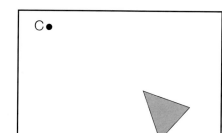

2. Work out the areas of these shapes.
Give your answer to 1 decimal place.

a)

9.8 m

12.5 m

b)

8.1 cm   12.4 cm

6.2 cm

....

C 3. A car travels 70 miles in 1 hour 20 minutes. Find the average speed in m.p.h.

....

C 4. A ladder of length 6 m rests so that the foot of the ladder is 3 m away from a wall.
Calculate how far up the wall the ladder reaches. Give your answer to 2 s.f.

125 cm

Express Oil   1.58 m

....

C 5. Calculate the volume of the oil drum, clearly stating your units. Give your answer to 3 significant figures.

....

C 6. A ladder of length 12 m rests against a wall in such a way that the angle which the ladder makes with the wall is 40°.
Calculate the height of the ladder above the ground,
giving your answer to 1 decimal place.

ladder   40°

....

C 7. In the diagram MN is parallel to YZ, YMX and ZNX are straight lines, XM = 5.1 cm, XY = 9.5 cm, XN = 6.3 cm, YZ = 6.8 cm. ∠YXZ = 29°, ∠XZY = 68°

a) What is the size of angle XNM ....

b) Calculate the length of MN ....
....

c) Calculate the length of XZ ....
....

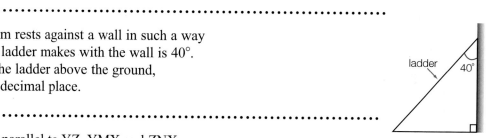

X

5.1 cm   6.3 cm

9.5 cm

M   N

Y   68°   Z

6.8 cm

8. Here are some expressions:

$7r^2t$	$1\sqrt{r^2+t^2}$	$\dfrac{rtl}{4}$	πr^2	$2\sqrt{r^2+t^2}$	$2tl$	$4\dfrac{r^3}{t^2}$

The letters r, t and l represent lengths. π, 2, 4 and 7 are numbers that have no dimensions.
Three of the expressions represent surface area. Tick the boxes (✓) underneath these three expressions.

C Indicates that a calculator may be used

C 9. Find the arc length and sector area of

5 cm
55°
5 cm

....

C 10. Find the volume of this metal container.

6 cm
20 cm   8 cm

....

C 11. The volume of this cone is 500 cm³.
Calculate the length of the radius.

30 cm
r

....

C 12. The surface area of a cone is 120 cm². What is the surface area of a similar cone which is four times as high?

....

C 13. The two spheres are similar. If the volume of the larger sphere is 2145 cm³ to
4 s.f., calculate the volume of the smaller sphere.

3 cm   8 cm

....

14. The diagram shows a triangle RST. B is the midpoint of RT and A is the point on RS such that AS = 2RA.
If $\overrightarrow{RA}$ = **r** and $\overrightarrow{RB}$ = **t**

a) Write $\overrightarrow{AB}$ in terms of **r** and **t**

R
r   t
A   B
                T
S

....

b) Write $\overrightarrow{AT}$ in terms of **r** and **t**

....

c) Write down $\overrightarrow{ST}$ in terms of **r** and **t**.

....

C 15. Work out all the solutions of 2cos X = 1 for values of X between −360° ⩽ X ⩽ 360°.

....

C 16. Work out the lettered side or angle in these triangles.

a)
80°   9 m
46°
x

b)
12 m   x   13 m
24 m

....

c)
12.6 m   9.4 m
72
x

d)
6 cm   80°   5 cm
x

....

....

C 17. In the diagram AB represents a vertical tower on level ground. R and S are two
points due west of B. The distance RS is 50 m. The angles of elevation of A from
S and R are 40° and 60° respectively.

Calculate the height in metres of the tower, AB.

A
40°   60°
S   50 m   R   B

....

18. Find the size of the lettered angles:

(a)   (b)   (c)

b
O
70°
a

a
b   122°
105°

b
a
62°   85°

a
110°
b

....

....

How did you do?

1–5	correct	....start again
6–11	correct	....getting there
12–14	correct	....good work
15–18	correct	....excellent

TYPES OF DATA

There are two main types of data:

QUANTITATIVE
the answer is a number,
e.g. how many blue cars
in a car park?

QUALITATIVE
the answer is a word,
e.g. what is your
favourite colour?

QUANTITATIVE data can be discrete or continuous:

- **Discrete data:** has an exact value. Each category is separate and is usually found by counting. Examples include the number of people with brown hair.

- **Continuous data:** here the values change from one category to the next. Examples include the heights and weights of students. Continuous data cannot be measured exactly. The accuracy of the measurement relies on the accuracy of the measuring equipment.

- **Primary data:** this is data which is collected by the person who is going to analyse and use it.

- **Secondary data:** this is data which is available from an external source, such as books, newspapers and the internet.

COLLECTING DATA

The census is one of the largest surveys that takes place. The census is done every 10 years and its main aim is to give a 'snapshot' of Britain today. In order to carry out the census all households are given a survey to complete.

HYPOTHESES AND EXPERIMENTS

A hypothesis is a prediction which can be tested. Experiments can be used to test hypotheses.

EXAMPLE

Hypothesis: The better the light, the faster seedlings grow.

Variable: This is the intensity of the light that can be changed.

Conditions: The other conditions must stay the same. All seedlings must be exactly the same size, strength and colour to start with. If there is bias (e.g. if one side of the tray gets extra sunlight), then the experiment needs to start again.

QUESTIONNAIRES

These can be used to test hypotheses.

WHEN DESIGNING QUESTIONNAIRES:
✔ Decide what needs to be found out: the <u>hypothesis</u>.
✔ Give instructions on how the questionnaire has to be filled in.
✔ Do not ask for information which is not needed (e.g. name).
✔ Make the questions clear and concise.

✔ Keep the questionnaire short.
✔ If people's opinions are needed, make sure the question is <u>unbiased</u>. An example of a biased question would be:

'Do you agree that a leisure centre should have a tennis court rather than a squash court?'

✔ Allow for any possible answers, for example:
Which of these is your favourite colour?

Examiner's Top Tip
When asked to design a questionnaire, always word the questions carefully. Try to avoid bias appearing in your questions.

Red	Blue	Green	Yellow	Other
☐	☐	☐	☐	☐

SAMPLING

This is an efficient way of collecting information about a population. It is important that the sample is representative of the population and does not contain bias.

There are three main methods of sampling.

The bigger the sample the more accurate the results

1. Random Sampling
In a random sample each member of the population has an equal chance of being chosen.

2. Stratified Sampling
Usually the population is divided into groups (strata) which have something in common e.g. age. A simple random sample is then taken from each group. The number in each sample is proportional to the size of the group.

3. Selective Sample
This is where every nth item is chosen and the value of n is selected at random.

- -

QUICK TEST

1. Design a questionnaire you could give a friend in order to find out what they do in their spare time.

2. Lucy is carrying out a survey on homework; she decides to use a stratified sample and ask 100 students. Calculate the number of students she will ask from each group.

	Frequency
Year 7	120
Year 8	150
Year 9	230

DRAWING PIE CHARTS

- These are used to illustrate data. They are circles split up into sections, each section representing a certain number of items.

EXAMPLE

The favourite sports of 24 students in year 11:

Sport	Frequency	Angle	Workings
Football	9	135°	$\frac{9}{24}$ x 360°
Swimming	5	75°	$\frac{5}{24}$ x 360°
Netball	3	45°	$\frac{3}{24}$ x 360°
Hockey	7	105°	$\frac{7}{24}$ x 360°
Total	24	360°	

To calculate the angles for the pie chart:
- Find the total for the items listed.
- Find the fraction of the total for each item.
- Multiply the fraction by 360° to find the angle.

Football 135°
Swimming 75°
Netball 45°
Hockey 105°

Key in on the calculator:
9 ÷ 24 ✕ 360 =

INTERPRETING PIE CHARTS

EXAMPLE

The pie chart shows how some students travel to school.

There are 18 students in total.

How many travel by:

a) Car?

b) Bus?

c) Foot?

Bus 80°
Car 60°
Foot 220°

360° = 18 students

1° = $\frac{18}{360}$ = 0.05 (work out 1°)

Car = 60° x 0.05 = 3 students

Bus = 80° x 0.05 = 4 students

Foot = 220° x 0.05 = 11 students

HISTOGRAMS

- These are drawn to illustrate <u>continuous data</u>. They are similar to bar charts except that there are no gaps between the bars. The data must be grouped into <u>equal</u> class intervals if the length of the bar is used to represent the frequency.

EXAMPLE

The weights of 30 workers in a factory are shown in the table:

Weight (kg)	Frequency
$45 \leq W < 55$	7
$55 \leq W < 65$	13
$65 \leq W < 75$	6
$75 \leq W < 85$	4

- $45 \leq W < 55$, etc, are called <u>class intervals</u> – notice they are all equal in width. This means the weights are between 45 and 55 kg. A weight of 55 kg would be in the next group.

Histogram showing weights of factory workers

NOTE:
- The axes do not need to start at zero.
- The axes are labelled.
- The graph has a title.

REPRESENTING DATA

FREQUENCY POLYGONS

To draw a frequency polygon join the <u>midpoints</u> of <u>class</u> <u>intervals</u> for grouped or continuous data. Consider the histogram of the factory workers again.
- Put a cross on the middle of each bar and join the crosses up with a ruler.
- Draw a line down from the middle of the first and last bar to the x axis to form a closed polygon, OR
- To form an open polygon do not join to the x axis.

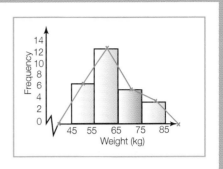

LINE GRAPHS

> This example is known as a time series because the data is recorded at intervals of time

- These are a set of points joined by lines.

Year	1988	1989	1990	1991	1992	1993
Number of cars sold	2500	2900	2100	1900	1600	800

- <u>Middle</u> <u>values</u>, like point A, have no meaning. A does not mean that halfway between 1990 and 1991, there were 2000 cars sold.

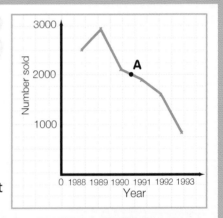

QUICK TEST

1. For this set of data, draw a pie chart.

Hair colour	Frequency
Brown	8
Auburn	4
Blonde	6
Black	6

2. Using the histogram: a) complete the frequency table below.

Height (cm)	Frequency
$140 \leq h < 145$	
$145 \leq h < 150$	10
$150 \leq h < 155$	
$155 \leq h < 160$	
$160 \leq h < 165$	

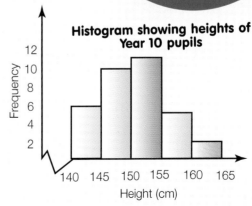

Histogram showing heights of Year 10 pupils

b) How many people were in the survey?

c) Draw a frequency polygon on the histogram.

1. The angles for the pie chart are: Brown 120°, Auburn 60°, Blonde 60°, Black 90° 2. a) The frequencies for the heights are: $140 \leq h < 145 = 6$, $145 \leq h < 150 = 10$, $150 \leq h < 155 = 11$, $155 \leq h < 160 = 5$, $160 \leq h < 165 = 2$ b) 34 people were in the survey c) The frequency polygon should be plotted at the midpoints of the bars

TYPES OF CORRELATION

There are three types of correlation:

POSITIVE	NEGATIVE	ZERO

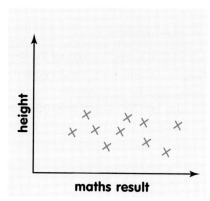

Positive
This is when both variables are increasing. If the points are nearly in a straight line there is said to be high positive correlation.

Negative
This is when one variable increases as the other decreases. If the points are nearly in a straight line it is said to have a high negative correlation.

Zero
This is when there is little or no correlation between the variables.

DRAWING A SCATTER DIAGRAM

- Work out the scales first.
- Plot the points carefully.
- Each time a point is plotted, tick it off.

EXAMPLE

Maths test (%)	64	79	38	42	49	75	83	82	66	61	54
History test (%)	70	36	84	70	74	42	29	33	50	56	64

The table shows the Maths and History test results of 11 pupils.

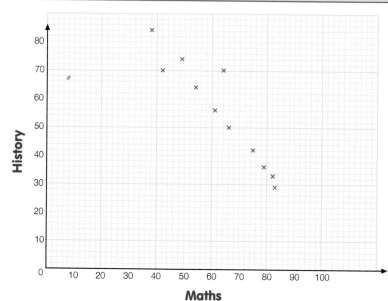

The scatter diagram shows that there is a strong negative correlation – in general, the better the pupils did in Maths, the worse they did in History and vice versa.

LINES OF BEST FIT

- <u>This is the line which best fits the data</u>. It goes in the direction of the data and has roughly the same number of points above the line as below it.
- A line of best fit can be used to make predictions.

EXAMPLE

If Hassam was away for a Maths test but got 78% in History then from the scatter diagram we can estimate he would have got approximately 44% in Maths.

Go to 78% on the History scale. Read across to the line then down.

Scatter diagram showing Maths and History marks

SCATTER DIAGRAMS AND CORRELATION

- A SCATTER DIAGRAM (SCATTER GRAPH OR SCATTER PLOT) IS USED TO SHOW TWO SETS OF DATA AT THE SAME TIME.

- ITS IMPORTANCE IS TO SHOW THE <u>CORRELATION</u> (CONNECTION) BETWEEN TWO SETS OF DATA.

Examiner's Top Tip
Do not rush when drawing a scatter diagram. Plot the points very carefully. Remember to show on your graph how you made your estimates.

QUICK TEST

1. For each pair of variables write down what type of correlation there is:

   a) Number of pages in a magazine and the number of advertisements

   b) The heights of students in a year group and the marks in the Maths test

   c) The height up a mountain and the temperature

   d) The age of a used car and its value

1. a) Positive b) Zero c) Negative d) Negative

AVERAGES ①

'Average height of students is 163 cm'

AVERAGES OF DISCRETE DATA

Do not round off

There are three types of average: mean, median and mode.
Mean: Sometimes known as the 'average'. The symbol for the mean is $\bar{x}$.

> **Mean = sum of a set of values** / **the number of values used**

Median: The middle value when the values are put in order of size.
Mode: The one that occurs the most often.
Range: This tells us how much the information is spread.
It is the highest value – lowest value.

EXAMPLE
A football team scored the following number of goals in their first 10 matches:
2, 4, 0, 1, 2, 2, 3, 6, 2, 4
Find the mean, median, mode and range of the number of goals scored.

Mean = $\frac{2 + 4 + 0 + 1 + 2 + 2 + 3 + 6 + 2 + 4}{10}$ = $\frac{26}{10}$ = 2.6 goals

Median = 0, 1, 2, 2, 2, 2, 3, 4, 4, 6   Put in order of size

0̸ 1̸ 2̸ 2̸ (2 2) 3̸ 4̸ 4̸ 6̸   Cross off from the ends to find the middle.

$\frac{2 + 2}{2}$ = 2 goals

> If there are 2 numbers in the middle the median is halfway between them.

Mode = 2 goals because it occurs 4 times.

Range = 6 – 0 = 6

FINDING A MISSING VALUE WHEN GIVEN THE MEAN

If you are given the mean of a set of discrete data you can use the information to calculate a missing value.

EXAMPLE
The mean of 15, 17, y, 28 and 19 is 16.
What is the value of y?

mean = $\frac{15 + 17 + y + 28 + 19}{5}$

$16 = \frac{79 + y}{5}$

so 16 x 5 = 79 + y

80 = 79 + y

so y = 80 – 79

y = 1

> This just becomes a simple equation to solve.

FINDING AVERAGES FROM A FREQUENCY TABLE

- A frequency table tells us how many are in a group.

EXAMPLE

Number of sisters (X)	0	1	2	3	4
Frequency (f)	4	9	3	5	2

This means 2 people had 4 sisters.

If there are two numbers in the middle, the median is halfway between them.

$$\text{Mean } (\bar{X}) = \frac{\Sigma fX}{\Sigma f}$$

$$= \frac{(4 \times 0) + (9 \times 1) + (3 \times 2) + (5 \times 3) + (2 \times 4)}{4 + 9 + 3 + 5 + 2 + 0}$$

$$= \frac{38}{23} = 1.7 \text{ (to 1 d.p.)}$$

Median   Since there are 23 people who have been asked the median will be the 12th person.

11 people   12   11 people

The 12th person has 1 sister ∴ the median = 1

Mode   This is the one with the highest frequency, that is 1 sister.

Range   4 − 0 = 4

Σ means the sum of

Examiner's Top Tip
When finding the mean from a frequency table try to remember to divide by the sum of the frequencies and not by how many groups there are.

MOVING AVERAGES

These are used to smooth out the changes in a set of data that varies over a period of time. A four-point moving average uses four data items in each calculation, a three point moving average uses three and so on.

A moving average can often give a good idea of any trend shown in a set of data as well as enabling you to draw a trend line on a time series graph.

EXAMPLE
Find the three-point moving average for the following data.
2, 4, 0, 1, 2, 2, 3, 6, 2, 4.
Average for 1st 3 data points $(2 + 4 + 0) \div 3 = 2$
Average for data points $(2 \to 4)$ $(4 + 0 + 1) \div 3 = 1.\dot{6}$
and so on …
$(0 + 1 + 2) \div 3 = 1$
$(1 + 2 + 2) \div 3 = 1.\dot{6}$
$(2 + 2 + 3) \div 3 = 2.\dot{3}$
$(2 + 3 + 6) \div 3 = 3.\dot{6}$
$(3 + 6 + 2) \div 3 = 3.\dot{6}$
$(6 + 2 + 4) \div 3 = 4$

QUICK TEST

1. Find the mean, median, mode and range of this set of data: 2, 9, 3, 6, 4, 4, 5, 8, 4

2. Charlotte made this table for the number of minutes students were late for registration

Number of minutes late (x)	0	1	2	3	4
Frequency (f)	10	4	6	3	2

Calculate:

a) the mean   b) the median   c) the mode   d) the range

1. mean = 5; median = 4; mode = 4; range = 7   2. a) mean = 1.32 mins b) median = 1 c) mode = 0 d) range = 4

TYPICAL GCSE QUESTION

Finding the mean of grouped data is a very common GCSE question and is usually worth about 4 marks.

EXAMPLE

The weight of some Year 9 pupils is shown below:

Weight (kg)	Frequency (f)	Midpoint (x)	fx
40 ≤ W < 45	7	42.5	297. 5
45 ≤ W < 50	4	47.5	190
50 ≤ W < 55	3	52.5	157.5
55 ≤ W < 60	1	57.5	57.5

Adding on these columns helps show your working out.

This is the same as on page 95 except the frequency is multiplied by the <u>midpoint</u>.

$$\underline{\text{Mean}} \quad = \frac{\Sigma fx}{\Sigma f} = \frac{(7 \times 42.5) + (4 \times 47.5) + (3 \times 52.5) + (1 \times 57.5)}{7 + 4 + 3 + 1}$$

$$= \frac{702.5}{15} = 46.8 \text{ kg (1 d.p.)}$$

<u>Modal class</u> = 40 ≤ W < 45

Examiner's Top Tip
If your calculator will do statistic[s] learn how to use it. It is much quicker but always do it twice a check. Always try and sho[w] full working out in order to obtain some method marks.

STEM AND LEAF DIAGRAMS

Stem and leaf diagrams are another way of recording information and they can be used to find the mode, median and range of a set of data.

EXAMPLE

Here are some marks gained by some students in a mathematics exam.

24	61	55	36	42
32	60	51	38	58
55	52	47	55	55

When the information is put into a stem and leaf diagram it looks like this:

Stem is 30 leaf is 2 ∴ 32

stem	leaf
2	4
3	② 6 8
4	2 7
5	1 2 5 5 5 5 8
6	0 1

Stem = 10 marks

To read off the values you multiply the stem by 10 and add on the leaf. Using the stem and leaf the mode, median and range can be found easily:

mode = 55
median = 52
range = 61 – 24
= 37

Stem and leaf diagrams are useful when comparing two sets of data.

USING AVERAGES AND SPREAD TO COMPARE DISTRIBUTIONS

Be careful when drawing conclusions from averages as they do not always tell the whole story.

EXAMPLE

11A obtained a mean of 57% in a test.

11T obtained a mean of 84% in the same test.

From the averages we would say that 11T is better than 11A. However if the range is looked at for each class:

11A = 100% – 21% = 79%

11T = 94% – 76% = 18%

Using the range it can be seen that not all of 11T are better than 11A, because some of 11A obtained higher marks than 11T.

The average of 11A has been lowered because of the low marks obtained by some pupils.

AVERAGES OF GROUPED DATA

- When the data are grouped into class intervals, the exact data are not known.
- Estimate the mean by using the <u>midpoint</u> of the <u>class interval</u>.
- The midpoint is the halfway value.
- When using grouped (continuous) data only the <u>modal</u> <u>class</u> can be found.
  This is the one with the highest frequency.

AVERAGES ②

USING APPROPRIATE AVERAGES

- The <u>mean </u>is useful when a 'typical' value is wanted.
  Be careful not to use the mean if there are extreme values.
- The <u>median</u> is a useful average to use if there are extreme values.
- The <u>mode</u> is useful when the most common value is needed.

QUICK TEST

1. The heights of some Year 10 pupils are shown in the table:

Height	Frequency
$140 \leq h < 145$	4
$145 \leq h < 150$	7
$150 \leq h < 155$	14
$155 \leq h < 160$	5
$160 \leq h < 165$	2

a) Calculate an estimate for the mean of this data.

b) Write down the modal class.

TYPICAL GCSE QUESTION

Ahmed carried out a survey for his Geography coursework. He recorded the distance that 200 people travelled to an out-of-town shopping centre. The table shows his findings.

Distance (d miles)	Frequency	Distance (d miles)	Cumulative Frequency
$0 \leq d < 5$	12	$0 \leq d < 5$	12
$5 \leq d < 10$	49	$0 \leq d < 10$	61
$10 \leq d < 15$	57	$0 \leq d < 15$	118
$15 \leq d < 20$	45	$0 \leq d < 20$	163
$20 \leq d < 25$	34	$0 \leq d < 25$	197
$25 \leq d < 30$	3	$0 \leq d < 30$	200

- To complete the cumulative frequency table the frequencies need to be added, e.g. 12 + 49 = 61.
- To check the cumulative frequency table is correct, the final value in the cumulative frequency column should be the same as the number of people in the survey.
- Plot (5, 12), (10, 61), etc. The **upper class** boundaries are used.
- Since no people had less than zero distance, the graph starts at (0, 0).
- Join the points with a smooth curve.

Examiner's Top Tip

Cumulative frequency graphs are one of the most common topics tested on the GCSE Intermediate/Higher level examination. Remember to:
- Draw graphs as accurately as possible. Try to avoid bumpy curves.
- Check your graph looks like an S shape.
- Plot the upper class boundaries
- Show the method lines for the median, etc. on your graphs.

BOX AND WHISKER DIAGRAMS

All cumulative frequency graphs tend to have the same basic shape so they are not easy to compare.

A box and whisker diagram shows the interquartile range as a box, this then makes it useful when comparing distributions.

The box and whisker diagram for the cumulative frequency graph above would look like this:

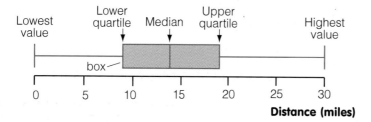

FINDING THE INTERQUARTILE RANGE

The interquartile range is found by subtracting the lower quartile from the upper quartile.

• <u>Interquartile range</u> = upper quartile − lower quartile
• <u>Upper quartile</u> This is the value three quarters of the way into the distribution.
   So $\frac{3}{4} \times 200 = 150$ approx. 18.7 miles for our data.
• <u>Lower quartile</u> This is the value one quarter of the way into the distribution.
   So $\frac{1}{4} \times 200 = 50$ approx. 9 miles for our data.
   The interquartile range for our data is $18.7 - 9 = 9.7$ miles.

FINDING THE MEDIAN

The median is the middle value of the distribution.
For the distance data:
Median = $\frac{1}{2}$ × total cumulative frequency = $\frac{1}{2} \times 200 = 100$

• Reading across from 100 to the graph and then down
  gives a median distance of about 13.4 miles.

CUMULATIVE FREQUENCY GRAPHS

These are very useful for finding the median and the spread of grouped data.

USING THE INTERQUARTILE RANGE

A large interquartile range indicates that the 'middle half' of the data is widely spread about the median.

A small interquartile range indicates that the 'middle half' of the data is concentrated about the median.

QUICK TEST

On another day Bethany also carried out the same survey. Her results are as follows:

Distance (d miles)	Frequency
$0 \leq d < 5$	15
$5 \leq d < 10$	60
$10 \leq d < 15$	67
$15 \leq d < 20$	30
$20 \leq d < 25$	22
$25 \leq d < 30$	6

1. Draw a cumulative frequency graph on the grid above.

2. Work out:
   a) the median
   b) interquartile range for this data.

2.a) Median approx. 12 miles
b) interquartile range = 9 miles (approx)

HISTOGRAMS

A histogram is similar to a bar chart except that bars can be of different widths.

DRAWING HISTOGRAMS

When the width of the columns are different the vertical axis is called the *FREQUENCY DENSITY* where

$$\text{frequency density} = \frac{\text{frequency}}{\text{class width}}$$

Hence the area of the rectangles are then proportional to the frequencies they represent.

Add an extra column, in order to work out frequency density

EXAMPLE

The table shows the distance travelled to school by some pupils.
Use the information to draw a histogram for this distribution.

Distance (km)	Frequency	Frequency density
$0 \leqslant d < 2$	12	$\frac{12}{2} = 6$
$2 \leqslant d < 4$	8	$\frac{8}{2} = 4$
$4 \leqslant d < 8$	10	$\frac{10}{4} = 2.5$
$8 \leqslant d < 16$	8	$\frac{8}{8} = 1$
$16 \leqslant d < 20$	6	$\frac{6}{4} = 1.5$

INTERPRETING HISTOGRAMS

Sometimes in an exam you are given a histogram and you are asked to use the information given in it to complete the frequency table.

In order to do this it is best to find the area of each bar and try and work out what one square equals. The rest should then be quite straightforward.

EXAMPLE

The histogram gives information about the ages of some runners in the 'Hillbilly' marathon. Use the information in the histogram to complete the table

Age (A) years	frequency
$0 \leqslant A < 20$	10
$20 \leqslant A < 30$	30
$30 \leqslant A < 40$	45
$40 \leqslant A < 60$	60
$60 \leqslant A < 100$	48

frequency = frequency density × class widths

Using this information the rest of the table can be filled in, shown in red.

Examiner's Top Tip
This is not a very difficult topic as long as you remember what frequency density is. This topic is a common one – quite often you are asked to interpret and complete a histogram all in one question.

QUICK TEST

Draw a histogram for the following information

Number of hours (h)	frequency
$0 \leqslant h < 20$	40
$20 \leqslant h < 30$	5
$30 \leqslant h < 60$	15
$60 \leqslant h < 70$	10
$70 \leqslant h < 100$	15

STANDARD DEVIATION

The standard deviation of a set of data is a measure of how far from the mean the data is spread.

CALCULATING STANDARD DEVIATION OF DISCRETE DATA

The standard deviation s, of a set of data is given by one of these two formulae: -

$$s = \sqrt{\frac{\Sigma(x - \bar{x})^2}{n}} \quad \text{or} \quad s = \sqrt{\frac{\Sigma x^2}{n} - \left(\frac{\Sigma x}{n}\right)^2}$$

Either of these two formulae can be used.

(note that $\frac{\Sigma x}{n}$ is the same as the mean)

EXAMPLE

Find the mean and standard deviation of these numbers 1, 1, 2, 3, 4, 5, 5

1) First work out the mean $\bar{x} = \frac{\Sigma x}{n} = \frac{1 + 1 + 2 + 3 + 4 + 5 + 5}{7} = \frac{21}{7} = 3$

2) Work out $\Sigma x^2 = 1^2 + 1^2 + 2^2 + 3^2 + 4^2 + 5^2 + 5^2 = 81$

3) Now substitute into the formula $\quad s = \sqrt{\frac{\Sigma x^2}{n} - \left(\frac{\Sigma x}{n}\right)^2} \quad s = \sqrt{\frac{81}{7} - (3)^2} \quad s = 1.6 \, (1dp)$

so the mean = 3 and the standard deviation s = 1.6

CALCULATING STANDARD DEVIATION OF GROUPED DATA

When calculating the standard deviation of grouped data, the two formulae have to be changed slightly.

$$s = \sqrt{\frac{\Sigma f(x - \bar{x})^2}{\Sigma f}} \quad \text{or} \quad s = \sqrt{\frac{\Sigma fx^2}{\Sigma f} - \left[\frac{\Sigma fx}{\Sigma f}\right]^2}$$

$(5^2 \times 9)$
$(15^2 \times 10)$

EXAMPLE

The frequency table shows the length of some leaves, l cm.

length of leaves (l cm)	frequency (f)	midpoint(x)	f(x)	fx²
$0 \leqslant l < 10$	9	5	45	225
$10 \leqslant l < 20$	10	15	150	2250
$20 \leqslant l < 30$	12	25	300	7500
$30 \leqslant l < 40$	4	35	140	4900

$\Sigma f = 35$ $\qquad\qquad \Sigma fx = 635 \quad \Sigma fx^2 = 14875$

$$s = \sqrt{\frac{\Sigma fx^2}{\Sigma f} - \left[\frac{\Sigma fx}{\Sigma f}\right]^2} \qquad s = \sqrt{\frac{14875}{35} - \left(\frac{635}{35}\right)^2}$$

$s = \sqrt{425 - (18.143)^2}$

$s = \sqrt{95.83...}$

$s = 9.7879...$

$s = 9.79 \, (2dp)$

Examiner's Top Tip
Standard deviation is no longer on the examination paper. However, you may wish to use this technique when completing your data handling project, as it gives you a good idea as to how spread out the data is from the mean

QUICK TEST

Calculate the mean and standard deviation of:

1. 2, 7, 1, 4, 1, 5, 6, 3

2. 9, 4, 7, 2, 1, 1, 4, 9, 6

KEY POINTS ABOUT STANDARD DEVIATION

1) The bigger the standard deviation the bigger the spread of the values from their mean, hence the less consistent the data.

2) For a set of data $(x_1, x_2, ... x_n)$ with mean $\bar{x}$ and standard deviation s then the mean and standard deviation of the data $(ax_1 \, ax_2 ... ax_n)$ is mean = $a\bar{x}$, standard deviation = as

3) For a set of data $(x_1, x_2 ... x_n)$ with mean $\bar{x}$ and standard deviation s, the mean and standard deviation of the data $(x_1 + a_1, x_2 + a, x_3 + a ... x_n + a)$ is mean = $\bar{x} + a$, standard deviation = s.

1. Mean = 3.625   s = 2.1176
2. Mean = 4.77   s = 2.973

WHAT IS PROBABILITY?

Probability is the chance or likelihood that something will happen.
All probabilities lie between 0 and 1.

0 — Definitely will not happen / Unlikely to happen — 0.5 — Very likely to happen / Definitely will happen — 1

Exhaustive _events_ account for all possible outcomes.
For example, the list HH, HT, TH, TT gives all possible outcomes
when two coins are tossed simultaneously.
Mutually _exclusive_ events are events that cannot happen at the same time.
For example if two students are chosen at random:

Event A: one student has brown hair

Event B: one student wears glasses

} These are _not_ _mutually_ _exclusive_ because brown-haired students can wear glasses.

Probability of an event = $\dfrac{\text{number of ways an event can happen}}{\text{total number of outcomes}}$

P(event) is a shortened way of writing probability of an event.

Example
There are 6 blue, 4 yellow and 2 red beads in a bag.
John chooses a bead at random. What is the probability he chooses:

a) a red bead?

b) a yellow bead?

c) a blue, yellow or red bead?

d) a white bead?

a) P(red) = $\frac{2}{12}$ or $\frac{1}{6}$

b) P(yellow) = $\frac{4}{12}$ or $\frac{1}{3}$

c) P(blue, yellow or red) = $\frac{12}{12}$ = 1

d) P(white) = 0

PROBABILITY OF AN EVENT NOT HAPPENING

If two events are <u>mutually</u> <u>exclusive</u>, then
P(event will happen) = 1 – P (event will not happen)
or
P(event will not happen) = 1 – P (event will happen)

EXAMPLE
The probability that someone gets flu next winter is 0.42. What is the probability that they do not get flu next winter?
P(not get flu) = 1 – P (get flu)
= 1 – 0.42
= 0.58

EXAMPLE
The probability that it will rain on any given day in August is $\frac{3}{11}$. What is the probability that it will not rain?
P(not rain) = 1 – P (will rain)
= 1 – $\frac{3}{11}$
= $\frac{8}{11}$

RELATIVE FREQUENCIES

Relative frequencies can be used as an estimate of probability.
If it is not possible to calculate probability, an experiment is used to find the relative frequency.

Relative frequency of an event = number of times event occurred
                                  total number of trials

EXAMPLE
When a fair die was thrown 80 times a six came up 12 times.
What is the relative frequency of getting a six?

number of trials = 80   relative frequency = $\frac{12}{80}$ = 0.15
number of sixes = 12

Examiner's Top Tip
Probabilities must be written as a fraction, decimal or percentage. Probabilities can never be greater than 1.

PROBABILITY 1

EXPECTED NUMBER

EXAMPLE

If a fair die is thrown 300 times, approximately how many fives are likely to be obtained?

P(5) = $\frac{1}{6}$ x 300 = 50 fives

We multiply 300 by $\frac{1}{6}$ since a 5 is expected $\frac{1}{6}$ of the time.

EXAMPLE

The probability of passing a driving test at the first attempt is 0.65. If there are 200 people taking their test for the first time, how many do you expect to pass the test?

0.65 x 200 = 130 people

QUICK TEST

1. Write down an event that will have a probability of zero.

2. A box contains 3 salt 'n' vinegar, 4 cheese and 2 bacon flavoured packets
   of crisps. If a packet of crisps is chosen at random what is the probability that it is:
   a) salt 'n' vinegar?   b) cheese?   c) onion flavoured?

3. The probability that it will not rain tomorrow is $\frac{2}{9}$. What is the probability that it will rain tomorrow?

4. The probability of achieving a grade C in Mathematics is 0.48. If 500 students sit the exam
   how many would you expect to achieve a grade C?

5. When a fair die was thrown 200 times, a five came
   up 47 times. What is the relative
   frequency of getting a five?

5. $\frac{47}{200}$
4. 240
3. $\frac{7}{9}$
2. a) $\frac{1}{3}$ b) $\frac{4}{9}$ c) 0
1. Answers could be: I will get a 7 when I throw a die; or I will get a 4 when I throw a coin

THE MULTIPLICATION LAW

- **When two events are <u>independent</u> the outcome of the second event is not affected by the outcome of the first.**
- **If two or more events are <u>independent</u>, the probability of A and B and C . . . happening together is found by <u>multiplying</u> the separate probabilities.**

P(A and B and C . . .) = P(A) x P(B) x P(C) . . .

EXAMPLE
The probability that it will rain on any day in August is $\frac{3}{10}$. Find the probability that:
a) **it will rain on both 1 August and 3 August.**
b) **it will rain on 9 August but not 20 August.**

a) **P (rain and rain) = $\frac{3}{10}$ x $\frac{3}{10}$ = $\frac{9}{100}$**
b) **P (rain and not rain) = $\frac{3}{10}$ x $\frac{7}{10}$ = $\frac{21}{100}$**

THE ADDITION LAW

If two or more events are <u>mutually</u> <u>exclusive</u> the probability of A or B or C . . . happening is found by <u>adding</u> the probabilities.
P (A or B or C. . .)
= P(A) + P(B) + P(C) + . . .

EXAMPLE
There are 11 counters in a bag: 5 of the counters are red and 3 of them are white. Lucy picks a counter at random. Find the probability that Lucy's counter is either red or white.

$P(\text{red}) = \frac{5}{11}$ $P(\text{white}) = \frac{3}{11}$

P(red or white) = P(red) + P(white)

$\frac{5}{11} + \frac{3}{11} = \frac{8}{11}$ Red and white are mutually exclusive

Examiner's Top Tip
When answering questions that involve tree diagrams remember to:
• make sure that on each pair of branches the probabilities add up to 1
• multiply along the branches
• add the probabilities of there being more than one alternative, i.e. P(A or B).

TREE DIAGRAMS

These are another way of showing the possible outcomes of two or more events. They may be written horizontally or vertically.

EXAMPLE
In a class, the probability that a pupil will have his/her own television is $\frac{5}{7}$ and the probability that the pupil will have his/her own computer is $\frac{1}{4}$. These two events are independent.
Draw a tree diagram of this information.
• Draw the first branch which shows the probabilities of having televisions.
• Put the probabilities on the branches.
• Draw the second branches which show the probabilities of having computers.

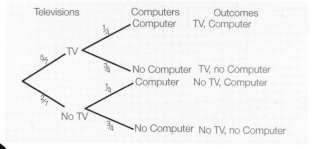

The multiplication and addition laws are useful when answering questions about tree diagrams.

a) Find the probability that a pupil will have their own TV and a computer.
P(TV and computer)   = P(TV) x P(computer)
= $\frac{5}{7}$ x $\frac{1}{4}$
= $\frac{5}{28}$

b) Find the probability that a pupil will have only one of the items.
P(TV and no computer) = P(TV) x P(no computer)
= $\frac{5}{7}$ x $\frac{3}{4}$
= $\frac{15}{28}$
OR
P(no TV and computer) = P(no TV) x P(computer)
= $\frac{2}{7}$ x $\frac{1}{4}$
= $\frac{2}{28}$

P(only one of the items)= $\frac{15}{28}$ + $\frac{2}{28}$ = $\frac{17}{28}$

SAMPLE SPACE DIAGRAMS

A table is helpful when considering outcomes of two events.
This kind of table is sometimes known as a <u>sample</u> <u>space</u> <u>diagram</u>.

EXAMPLE
Two dice are thrown together and their scores are added. Draw a diagram to show all the outcomes. Find the probability of:
a) a score of 7.
b) a score that is a multiple of 4.

a) $P(\text{score of } 7) = \frac{6}{36} = \frac{1}{6}$
b) $P(\text{multiple of } 4) = \frac{9}{36} = \frac{1}{4}$

	First die					
	1	2	3	4	5	6
1	2	3	4	5	6	7
2	3	4	5	6	7	8
Second die **3**	4	5	6	7	8	9
4	5	6	7	8	9	10
5	6	7	8	9	10	11
6	7	8	9	10	11	12

There are 36 outcomes.

PROBABILITY ②

QUICK TEST

1. The probability that Meena does her homework is 0.8. The probability that Fiona does her homework is 0.45. Find the probability that both girls do their homework.

2. a) Draw a sample space diagram which shows the outcomes when two dice are thrown together and their scores are multiplied.   b) What is the probability of a score of 6?
   c) What is the probability of a score of 37?

3. A bag contains 3 red and 4 blue counters. If a counter is taken out of the bag at random, its colour noted and then it is replaced, and a second counter is taken out, what is the probability of choosing one counter of each colour? (Hint: use a tree diagram to help you.)

1. 0.36
2. a)

	Die 1					
	1	2	3	4	5	6
1	1	2	3	4	5	6
2	2	4	6	8	10	12
Die 2 **3**	3	6	9	12	15	18
4	4	8	12	16	20	24
5	5	10	15	20	25	30
6	6	12	18	24	30	36

b) $\frac{4}{36} = \frac{1}{9}$ **c)** 0   **3.** $\frac{24}{49}$

EXAM QUESTIONS -

1. Michelle is a swimmer. The probability of her winning a race is 84%. If she swims in 50 races this season, how many races would you expect her to win?

....

2. A die is thrown and the scores are noted.
   The results are shown in this table:
   Work out the mean die score.

Die score	1	2	3	4	5	6
Frequency	12	15	10	8	14	13

....

3. In a survey the heights of ten girls and their shoe sizes were measured:

Height in cm	150	157	159	161	158	164	154	152	162	168
Shoe size	3	5	$5\frac{1}{2}$	6	5	$6\frac{1}{2}$	4	$3\frac{1}{2}$	6	7

a) Draw a scatter diagram to illustrate this data.
b) What type of correlation is there between height and shoe size?...
c) Draw a line of best fit on your diagram. ....
d) From your scatter diagram, estimate the height of a girl whose shoe size is $4\frac{1}{2}$. ....

4. The weights of some students in a class are measured.
These are the results
a) Work out an estimate for the mean weight of the students.

....

b) What is the modal class? ....

Weight in kg	Number of students
$40 \leqslant W < 45$	6
$45 \leqslant W < 50$	5
$50 \leqslant W < 55$	8
$55 \leqslant W < 60$	4
$60 \leqslant W < 65$	2

5. Ahmed and Matthew are going to take a swimming test.
   The probability that Ahmed will pass the swimming test is 0.85.
   The probability that Matthew will pass the swimming test is 0.6. The two events are independent.
a) Complete the probability tree diagram.
b) Work out the probability that both Ahmed and
   Matthew will pass the swimming test

....

c) Work out the probability that one of
   them will pass the swimming test and
   the other will not pass the swimming test

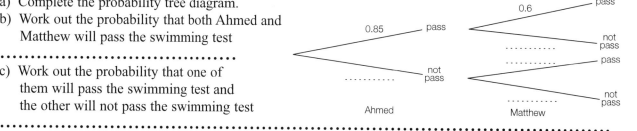

....

6. The table shows the time in minutes
   for 83 peoples' journeys to work.
a) Complete the cumulative frequency
   column in the table.
b) Draw a cumulative frequency graph of the data.
c) From your graph find the median.

....

d) From your graph find the interquartile range

Time in minutes	Frequency	Cumulative frequency
$0 \leqslant t < 10$	5	
$10 \leqslant t < 20$	20	
$20 \leqslant t < 30$	26	
$30 \leqslant t < 40$	18	
$40 \leqslant t < 50$	10	
$50 \leqslant t < 60$	4	

....

e) How many people had a journey of more than 45 minutes to work?

....

7. The table shows the working life hours (h) of 60 batteries.

Number of hours(h)	Frequency
$0 \leqslant h < 5$	9
$5 \leqslant h < 20$	15
$20 \leqslant h < 30$	18
$30 \leqslant h < 50$	10
$50 \leqslant h < 60$	8

Draw a histogram of this information.

(C) Indicates that a calculator may be used

8. A bag contains 4 red and 3 green beads. A bead is taken from the bag at random, and then replaced. A second bead is then taken. What is the probability that:

a) both beads are red

b) the beads are different colours.

....

....

9. There are 1200 pupils at a school. The table shows how they are distributed by year group.

Year	Number of pupils
7	180
8	265
9	245
10	210
11	300

Emily is conducting a survey about pupil's favourite sports. She decides to use a stratified random sample of 200 pupils. How many students in each year group does she need to sample?

....

The next two questions are to test your understanding of standard deviation but will not appear on the examination paper.

10. Calculate the mean and standard deviation of:

    1, 2, 3, 4, 5

....

b) Write down the mean and standard deviation of:

    $1 + a, 2 + a, 3 + a, 4 + a, 5 + a$

....

c) Write down the mean and standard deviation of:

    $1b, 2b, 3b, 4b, 5b$

....

11. Calculate the standard deviation of this frequency distribution.

χ	Frequency
1	10
2	5
3	7
4	4
5	6

....

....

c

How did you do?

1–3	correct	....start again
4–6	correct	....getting there
7–9	correct	....good work
10–11	correct	....excellent

EXAM QUESTIONS – Use the questions to test your progress. Check your answers on page 111.

1. Solve the following equations:
a) $2X - 4 = 10$ ....
b) $6X - 3 = 4X + 9$ ....
c) $5(2X + 1) = 20$ ....

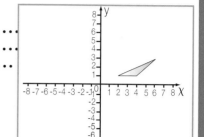

2. On the grid below, draw the image of the shaded shape after:
   a) A reflection in the line $y = X$. Call the image B.
   b) A rotation of $180°$ about the origin $(0, 0)$. Call the image C.
   c) A translation by the vector $\binom{-5}{4}$. Call the image D.

(c) 3. $s = ut + \frac{1}{2}at^2$. Calculate the value of s when $u = -6$, $t = 4.2$ and $a = \frac{5}{8}$.

....

4. The diagram shows a triangular prism. Work out the volume of the
   triangular prism, clearly stating your units.

....

(c) 5. £360 is invested for 3 years at 5% compound interest, which is paid annually.
   What is the total interest earned?

....

(c) 6. Using a trial and improvement method or otherwise solve the equation $t^3 - t = 15$.
Show full working out and give your answer to 1 decimal place.

....

(c) 7. The mass of an atom is 2×10^{-23} grams. What is the total mass of 9×10^{15} of these atoms?

....

(c) 8. Matthew and Emily are going to take a driving test. The probability that Matthew will pass the driving test
is 0.75. The probability that Emily will pass the driving test is 0.8. The two events are independent.

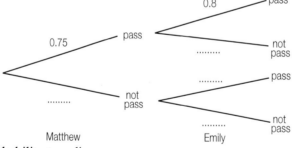

a) Complete the probability tree diagram.
b) Work out the probability that both Matthew and Emily
   will pass the driving test.

c) Work out the probability that one of them will pass the driving
   test and the other one will not pass the driving test.

....

(c) 9. ABCD is a quadrilateral. Angle DBA = $90°$, Angle DBC = $40°$, AB = 8 cm, BD = 6 cm.
a) Calculate the size of angle DAB. Give your answer correct to 3 s.f.

....
....

b) Calculate the length of DC. Give your answer correct to 2 s.f.

....
....

(c) Indicates that a calculator may be used

10. Solve $4^{k-1} = 8$

....

11. Two containers A and B are similar.
    The surface area of container A is 900 cm²
    The surface area of container B is 400 cm²
    The volume of A is 2200 cm³. Calculate the volume of container B.

....

12. Evaluate the following
a) 4^0 b) 5^{-2} c) $8^{2/3}$

....

13. y is inversely proportional to the square of x and y = 4 when x = 3.
a) Find a formula for y in terms of x.
b) Find the value of x when y = 3600

....

14 a) Factorise the following: i) $p^2 - q^2$ ii) $10x^2 - x - 2$

....

b) Solve the quadratic equation $3x^2 - 5x - 1 = 0$, giving your answer to 2 decimal places.

....

15. The diagram shows a field.
a) Calculate the length of BD.
b) Calculate the size of BĈD.
c) Work out the total area of the field.

16. A sack contains 60 apples. The frequency table gives information about the masses of these apples.
Draw a histogram to represent this information.

Mass (m) grams	Frequency
$0 \leqslant m < 100$	15
$100 \leqslant m < 150$	9
$150 \leqslant m < 250$	12
$250 \leqslant m < 300$	20
$300 \leqslant m < 400$	4

17. Simplify as far as possible

$$\frac{x^2 + 3x - 10}{x^2 - 4} \times \frac{x^2 + 5x + 6}{x^2 + 10x + 25}$$

....

18. The length and width of a rectangle are 22.3 cm and 9.2 cm (both correct to 1dp) respectively. Find the upper and lower bounds of the area of the rectangle.

How did you do?

1–5	correct	.......start again
6–10	correct	.......getting there
11–15	correct	.......good work
16–18	correct	.......excellent

Number

1. £25000

2. a) 365   b) 0.706

3. $\dfrac{9+9}{0.2\times50} = \dfrac{18}{10} = 1.8$

4. The 100 ml tube of toothpaste.

5. 1.5 cm

6. £376.47

7. £6502.50

8. £715.02

9. 20%

10. a) 2.67×10^6 b) 4.27×10^3
    c) 3.296×10^{-2} d) 2.7×10^{-2}

11. a) 4.2×10^{-5} g   b) 2.52×10^1 g

12. a) 1.2×10^{22} b) 2×10^{11}

13. $y = 3x$
    b) $x = 6.\dot{6}$

14. $y = \dfrac{20}{x^2}$,   a) $y = 1\frac{1}{4}$
    b) $x = \sqrt{2} = (1.414\ldots)$

15. a) $\dfrac{4}{9}$ b) $\dfrac{21}{99} = \dfrac{7}{33}$ c) $\dfrac{234}{999} = \dfrac{26}{111}$
    d) $\dfrac{25}{90} = \dfrac{5}{18}$

16. a) $2\sqrt{3}$ b) $5\sqrt{3}$ c) $10\sqrt{2}$ d) $3\sqrt{2} - 2\sqrt{6}$ e) 15

17. Upper bound = 2.301375 m²
    Lower bound = 2.271075 m²

18. Upper bound = 13.28 m/s (2dp)
    Lower bound = 13.04 m/s (2dp)

19. Upper bound = 6.7349 cm (4dp)
    Lower bound = 6.7112 cm (4dp)

20. a) 4 b) 4 c) $\dfrac{1}{36}$ d) 7 e) $\dfrac{1}{5}$ f) $\dfrac{1}{16}$ g) $\dfrac{49}{25}$

Algebra

1. a) $x = 3$ b) $x = 4$ c) $x = 5$ d) $x = 2$ e) $x = 1$

2. $2n^2 + 1$

3. a) $12x^4$ b) $12x^5 y^3$
   c) $4y^3$ d) $9y^4$

4. $a = 3$, $b = -2$

5. $P = 54.3$ (3 s.f.) b) $y = \dfrac{P^2 + 3x^2}{5x}$

6. $x = 1.8$

7. $1 \leqslant n \leqslant 3$

8. A is $(y = 3 - 4x)$ B is $(y = 2x + 1)$
   C is $(xy = 6)$ D is $(y = x^2 - 4)$

9. a) $\dfrac{5x + 8}{(x + 4)(x - 2)}$ b) $\dfrac{4x + 30}{(x - 3)(x + 4)}$ c) $\dfrac{1}{2}$

10. $(x - 2)(2x - 9) = 0$ $\therefore$ $x = 2$ $x = {}^9/_2$

11. a) $x = 1.721$, $x = -0.387$
    b) $x = 0.8385$, $x = -0.2385$

12. a) $(x - 2)^2 - 3 = 0$ b) $(x - 4)^2 - 6 = 0$
    $x = 3.732$ $x = 6.449$
    $x = 0.268$ $x = 1.551$

13. i) $(2x + 4)(x - 1) = 50$
    $2x^2 + 2x - 4 = 50$
    $2x^2 + 2x - 54 = 0$
    $x^2 + x - 27 = 0$
    ii) $x = 4.72$
    Length = 13.44 cm

14. $x = 0$ $y = 4$
    $x = -4$ $y = 0$
    The line $y = x + 4$ intersects the circle
    $x^2 + y^2 = 16$ at $(0, 4)$ and $(-4, 0)$.

15. $p = \dfrac{4x - 2r}{6 + x}$

16. a) Move graph 2 units to left.
    b) Move graph 3 units down the y axis.
    c) Reflect the graph in the x axis.
    d) Multiply all x values by 1/2.

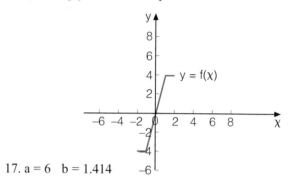

17. $a = 6$ $b = 1.414$

Shape, Space and Measures

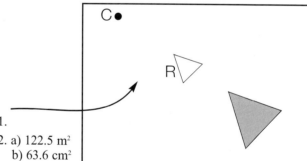

1.

2. a) 122.5 m²
   b) 63.6 cm²

3. 52.5 m.p.h.

4. 5.2 m

5. 1.94 m³

6. 9.2 m

7. a) 68°
   b) 3.65 cm
   c) 11.74 cm

8. 1 $\sqrt{r^2 + t^2}$; πr^2; 2tl

9. Arc length = 4.80 cm
   Sector area = 12.0 cm

10. Volume = 697.43 cm³

11. Radius = 3.99 cm (2dp)

12. Surface area = 1920 cm²

13. Volume = 113.1 cm³

14. a) $-\underline{r} + \underline{t}$ b) $-\underline{r} + 2\underline{t}$ c) $-3\underline{r} + 2\underline{t}$

15. -300 degrees, -60 degrees, 60 degrees, 300 degrees

16. a) 12.32 m (2dp)
b) $x = 147.5$ degrees (1dp)
c) $x = 45.2$ degrees (1dp)
d) $x = 7.11$ cm (2dp)

17. height = 81.4 m (1dp)

18.(1) $a = 55°$ $b = 35°$
   (2) $a = 75°$ $b = 58°$
   (3) $a = 85°$ $b = 62°$
   (4) $a = 55°$ $b = 70°$

Handling Data

1. 42 races

2. 3.5

3. a)

b) Positive correlation   c) See scatter diagram   d) 155.5 cm

4.   a) 50.7 kg   b) $50 \leqslant W < 55$

5.   a) 0.51
     b) 0.43

Ahmed   Matthew

6.a)

Time (mins)	Frequency	Cumulative frequency
$0 \leqslant t < 10$	5	5
$10 \leqslant t < 20$	20	25
$20 \leqslant t < 30$	26	51
$30 \leqslant t < 40$	18	69
$40 \leqslant t < 50$	10	79
$50 \leqslant t < 60$	4	83

b)
c) Approx 26 min
d) 18 min
e) 8 people

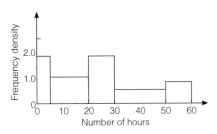

7.

8 a) $\frac{16}{49}$ b) $\frac{24}{49}$

9. Yr 7   30
   Yr 8   44
   Yr 9   41
   Yr 10   35
   Yr 11   50

10. a) Mean = 3
    Standard deviation = 1.414 (3dp)
    b) Mean = $3 + a$
    Standard deviation = 1.414 (3dp)
    c) Mean = $3b$
    Standard deviation = 1.414b

11. Standard deviation = 1.48396 = 1.48 (2dp)

Mixed

1. a) $X = 7$ b) $X = 6$ c) $X = \frac{3}{2}$ or 1.5

2.

3. -19.6875

4. 1080 cm³

5. £56.75

6. $t = 2.6$

7. 1.8×10^{-7} grams

8. a) See below
   b) 0.6
   c) 0.35

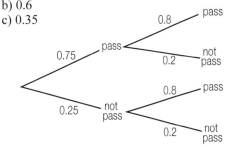

9. a) $36.87° = 36.9°$ (3 s.f.) b) 3.9 (2 s.f.)

10. $k = 2\frac{1}{2}$

11. 651.9 cm³

12. a) 1   b) $\frac{1}{25}$ c) 4

13. a) $y = \frac{36}{X^2}$ b) $X = \pm \frac{1}{10}$

14. a) i) $(p - q)(p + q)$
       ii) $(5X + 2)(2X - 1)$
    b) $X = 1.85$, $X = -0.18$

15. BD = 8.86 m
     Angle BCD = 36.1°
     Total area = 89.43 m²

16.

17. $\dfrac{(X + 3)}{(X + 5)}$

18. Lower bound = 203.5875 cm²
    Upper bound = 206.7375 cm²

INDEX